DOTTORE!

INTERNMENT IN ITALY, 1940-1945

DOTTORE!

Internment in Italy, 1940-1945

Dr. Salim Diamand

MOSAIC PRESS

Oakville — New York — London

CANADIAN CATALOGUING IN PUBLICATION DATA

Diamand, Salim, 1914-
    Dottore!

ISBN 0-88962-368-6 (bound) ISBN 0-88962-369-4 (pbk.)

1. Diamand, Salim, 1914-   . 2. World War, 1939-
1945 - Concentration camps - Italy. 3. World War,
1939-1945 - Personal narratives, Jewish. 4. World
War, 1939-1945 - Jews - Italy. 5. Physicians -
Italy - Biography. I. Title.

D805.I8D53 1987   940.54'72'450924   C87-094360-X

Published by Mosaic Press, P.O. Box 1032,
Oakville, Ontario, L6J 5E9, Canada. Offices
and warehouse at 1252 Speers Rd., Unit 10,
Oakville, Ontario, L6L 5N9, Canada.

Published with the assistance of the Canada
Council and the Ontario Arts Council.

Keyboarded by Mosaic Press
Typeset by Speed River Graphics
Printed and bound in Canada

ISBN   0-88962-368-6 cloth
        0-88962-369-4 paper

MOSAIC PRESS:

IN THE UNITED STATES:
    Riverrun Press Inc., 1170 Broadway, Suite
    807, New York, N.Y., 10001, U.S.A.
IN THE U.K.:
    John Calder (Publishers) Ltd., 18 Brewer
    Street, London, W1R 4AS, England.

THE EYEWITNESS SERIES

The Mosaic Press Eyewitness series is devoted to personal, eye-witness, first-hand accounts, analyses, memoirs of significant historical events.

ACKNOWLEDGEMENTS

Many people have assisted and inspired me to undertake the writing of this book. I especially owe a debt of thanks to my Family, Hilde, and Pepita, Cila Schatzberg, Dr. Allen Schatzberg, Drs. Hatterer, Frank Lucht. All my many Italian friends, my teachers and colleagues in the Medical Profession; Mr. Richard Shiff and his Family; Dr. L. Scafuri; M. Valenzi; Dr. Numeroso; Familia Urcioli; Stella Angela; Irving Abella; Howard Aster; the Scotti Family; B. and M. Ludwig. To these and countless other people who I have encountered in my lengthy medical practice I dedicate this book.

Toronto, May 1987

INTRODUCTION

What follows in these pages is a memoir about Italy, about a Jew in Italy during the Second World War. Most of the Holocaust literature is about Eastern Europe. I was one of those Eastern European Jews who managed to leave that part of Europe for western Europe before the war. I studied medicine in France and then in Italy. With the outbreak of the war in September, 1939, I found myself cut-off from my family and on my own in Italy.

The years of one's professional training, in my case medical studies, and then one's first professional years are always very important. These years, for me, took place in Italy. These years also coincided with the war years. For more than a decade, I lived, studied, worked and was also put in a concentration camp in Italy. And, in subsequent years, when I left Italy to take up medical practice in Canada, I continued to be closely, intimately associated with Italians and the Italian community. I can honestly say that I think I know Italians, how they think, what they feel, their attitudes, values, sentiments.

Throughout my years of confinement in various camps during the war years in Italy, I never found racism in Italians. Of course there was militarism; but throughout the war years, I never found any Italians who approached me, as a Jew, with the idea of exterminating my race.

In the pages which follow, you will find one man's story — how I survived during the war years in Italian concentration camps. Too little is known about Italian camps, about the conditions of these camps, about Jews in Italy during the war years. This short memoir is an attempt to kindle some interest in these matters, to provoke some concern in this era and in this part of Europe during the war. Everyone's life is unique in some way. Every story of survival during the Second World War is unique in its own way. For this reason alone, a memoir about one man's survival during the Second World War is worth noting for subsequent generations.

Dr. Salim Diamand

Chapter 1

THE ARREST

June 18, 1940, early morning. I awaken to a knocking at my door. I hastily put on an old pair of trousers and a jacket, open the door slightly, and see two policemen.

"You are Dottore Diamand, Dottore, Dottore?" one of them asks politely.

"Yes", I answer sleepily.

"Come with us, we need some information from you".

"I have to put on some decent clothes".

"No, it's only for a few minutes, you don't need to get dresssed properly".

I walk through a bright early Naples morning with two policemen to the station, a few minutes from my apartment.

I never returned to my apartment for my clothing.

At the time of my arrest I had just completed my medical education at the University of Naples. I was born in Bolechow in 1914 in the Austro-Hungarian Province of Galicia. The town, as many others in the area, had a largely Jewish population and was rich in Jewish history. This area, eastern Galicia, had a Ukrainian majority, a large Jewish minority as well as Poles, Hungarians and Germans. In my early years the area was fought over and contested by the polish Republic, Ukrainian nationalists, Communists and anti-Communists. Bolechow came under Polish rule after World War I and is today part of the U.S.S.R.

Growing up in this area I learned to speak Yiddish, Polish, German and Ukrainian. As Jews, we experienced the hostility of both the Poles and the Ukrainians. Even in peaceful times, Jews always sensed an undercurrent of hostility and turbulence that made us constantly uneasy.

Despite international guarantees and the assurances of the First President, Marshall Pilsudski during the inter-war period, the social, economic, and political position of Jews in this area deteriorated steadily. The public life of Poland became increasingly fired with anti-semitism. First, the Polish Parliament passed legislation that discriminated against Jews without every mentioning the word "Jew" and the Polish state failed to respect their treaty obligations to Jews as an ethnic minority.

In 1934 an overtly anti-semitic government took power. One of the first acts of the new regime was to impose a numerus clausus on admissions to universities, thus limiting the number of Jews. This meant only those Jewish students with near perfect grades could be admitted to university and it meant that a student, such as I, with better than average grades, who would normally be admitted to any respectable university, had to forego further education or look elsewhere.

My family, sensing the deteriorating condition of Jews, had already begun to look beyond Poland. One married sister had moved to Vienna. My parents and I decided that I should study medicine in another country. My father, a modestly prosperous leather merchant, was prepared to provide financial support for me.

In 1933, I want to Rheims, France. This part of France was a hotbed of xenophobia and feelings against all foreigners ran high. During a period of labour unrest, 20,000 Polish miners expressed their discontent about their working conditions in words and deeds. The local population, including the police, were unable to maintain order. There was a sense of imminent violence hovering around. I had been spending my first academic year in this environment and I felt insecure, uncertain about my future in Rheims. I completed the academic year and, during the summer months, I travelled to Pisa on holiday.

In Pisa, I felt totally different — comfortable, secure, welcome. I enjoyed the openness of the Italians, the respect for foreigners, the sense of security. I enrolled as a medical student in Pisa in 1934. Everyone knew that I was Jewish, but I sensed no anti-semitism. Indeed, I was able to apply myself to my medical studies and to feel that I was being treated equal to everybody else. I quickly learned to speak and read Italian and I was even able to master some of the local dialects.

The following September, 1935, I went to Genoa and continued my medical training. Again, I along with all the other foreign students felt secure and welcome. From September 1936 until June 1939, I continued my medical studies and training in Naples, a city I began to love as my true home.

The first cloud appeared on the horizon after Mussolini allied Italy formally with Germany and then enacted anti-Jewish laws. For many Italian Jews, whose ancestors had been in Italy for many centuries, who had supported the removal of foreign rule, unification and been active citizens, this was an almost unbearable shock. I knew of one who committed suicide as a result.

As a foreigner, the laws had little effect on my daily life. I was required to register as a Jew before an official who stated that he could not understand what it was all about and was apologetic about troubling us. All of this made no difference in my relationship with my professors, fellow students and friends, including a girl friend. Many of my friends were anti-Fascists, including Communists and Socialists, active in the illegal opposition to the government. As a foreigner, I kept myself apart from and uninvolved in any political activity.

World War II broke out in September 1939 and I soon lost

Dr. Salim Diamand

contact with my family in Poland. Italy remained nominally
neutral until June 10th, 1940. In December my sister and her
family managed to leave Vienna with an American visa. We had a
brief reunion in Naples, where they embarked for the United
States. We parted uncertain of what the future would hold.

Having completed my medical training, I had to decide how
to practice my profession. To my friends it seemed pointless for
me to take my examinations or "esame di stato", the license to
practice medicine in Italy, for the laws excluded Jews from
practice. Being optimistic, I chose to take the examination.
Therefore, in accordance with Italian law, I had to travel to
another city to be examined. I arranged to be examined in
Catania at the Victor Emanuelle Hospital. My examiners
included several world renowned physicians: Professor Citelli,
whose name appears in medical texts as the founder of the Citelli
Syndrome; and Professor Dolliotti who developed epidural
anaesthesia. I completed my examination and received a license.
Where and how would I practice medicine?

Italy declared war on June 10, 1940 and on June 18th I walked
in my half-dressed state through the streets of Naples. From that
fateful day onward I would practice medicine in ways and places
I had never anticipated!

At the station, the police took me to a room in which there
were 15 or 20 other persons. Most were familiar to me and were
doctors and medical students I had met in the course of my
studies. All were Jews — Polish, German, Hungarian and other
nationalities. We stood around for several hours, uncertain and
uneasy. We were told nothing of our destinations. After a few
hours they loaded us onto trucks and took us to the jail.

The jail was Italy's biggest, the Poggiorele. Built in Napoleon's
time, its walls were five feet thick with tiny slit windows. Its most
impressive quality was the amazing variety of insects that
crawled, climbed, bit, scratched and gave off a constant stream of
odours. After eight days our ordeal came to an end when our
belongings were returned to us and we were taken to the railway
station and put on a train.

Our next stop was Eboli, a town made internationally famous

14

by an earlier prisoner and physician — Carlo Levi. As an anti-Fascist he was exiled to a remote, forlorn village in the mountains overlooking the town and he wrote of the experience in his widely-read book Christ Stopped at Eboli. We did not go beyond Eboli for several months but we shared a similar type of imprisonment.

Our new imprisonment took on a pleasanter quality. We were housed in an old cassene, then a military barracks. The Carlabinieri were in charge, but they did not rule over us with a heavy hand. We received eight lira per day to meet our basic needs and we were free to move about the town until 6:00 p.m. We bought our food from the local people. Fortunately Eboli produced fine cheeses and food products and therefore we lived on our modest allowances.

The townspeople were indifferent to our status a Jews, or enemy aliens, or prisoners. We made friends among the local populace and the police. We met them in cafes, spent afternoon hours in conversation with them and we met them in football matches. Like tourists, we took pictures of the town and our new-found friends. Of course, we missed the variety and bustle of the big city, but it was a relaxing and healthy existence. If one must be a prisoner, then Eboli in the summer of 1940 was as good an incarceration as one might have hoped for.

But our stay in Eboli was temporary. Sadly, we left Eboli at the end of September. Now we numbered 100. We were loaded onto trucks heading for Calabria. We were being moved to a larger concentration camp which was being constructed.

We were the first group of prisoners to arrive at Farramonte which was Italy's largest concentration camp, built to house 2000 inmates. The camp was located in the Province of Cosenza, in the toe (or instep) of Italy. It was set in a fetid, swampy area along the Crati River, near the village of Tarsia. This camp was modelled after the pre-war German concentration camps with a barbed wire fence on its perimeter. The inmates were housed in u-shaped buildings. We slept in the arms of the "U" and the connecting portion served as kitchen, storeroom and washroom for both parts.

Dr. Salim Diamand

When we arrived, the construction and the furnishings of the camp were incomplete. The workmen of Perrini Construction were still at work and we had to gather straw on our first night in order to have something to sleep on.

Our first night brought us up against a peculiar combination of Italian hospitality and bureaucracy. Someone in Rome classified us as "English sympathizers" and, therefore, "tea-drinkers". As we were the "guests" of the Italian government, it was proper that we had an ample supply of tea. Italy in 1940, of course, was not a country of tea drinkers and tea was hard to find. But the eager government officials who looked after our interests managed to put together a large quantity of tea. Do we like tea? Do we want it? In truth, most of us despised the drink and we suffered with it until we found a way to obtain coffee.

While our tea supply was more than adequate, other inadequacies were present for most of our stay. The buildings were very simply made. In winter we felt the cold and dampness penetrating our bones and in summer they were hot and humid. The climate was very unpleasant. We felt the effects of the moisture given off by the swamp and there was dampness all around us.

The camp was under the control of the Carabiniere — the police and most of the guards were members of the Fascist Milizia. The Milizia were card-carrying members of the Fascist Party. We quickly learned that all but a few were ideologically oriented. Milizia duty assured them steady incomes, extra rations, and privileges for their families. Most of all, it exempted them from army call-up. Like the people in Eboli, our Milizia guards displayed no animosity toward us and we were able to establish warm and friendly relationships with many of them. Almost from the first, both guards and prisoners came to an implicit agreement: we would make as little trouble as possible for each other. Occasional bribes and other services helped to keep our guards happy. The Commandant, a Carabiniere officer, was also satisfied to have a docile, trouble-free camp.

There were a few, real Fascists. One of them was the first camp doctor, a man that no one trusted — neither prisoners nor guards. He was avoided as much as possible. The Commandant maneuvered to get rid of him and he was called up for service in the Army, at the Russian Front, we believed.

The camp filled up with new arrivals over several months. Most of the inmates were Jews from other countries. Occasionally, an Italian Jew showed up. One of them was a pediatrician whose family name was Stock, a scion of the family that owned the largest liqueur distilling company in Italy. There were others who more properly belonged in a mental hospital!

One day a group of Greeks, non-Jews, were brought into the camp. Their arrival contrasted sharply with the way we Jews had come. These Greeks were rounded up during Italy's abortive invasion of Greece. They came to the camp in chains, each prisoner accompanied by two Carabiniere. At first they were closely guarded until they came to realize that escape into the swamps and the desolate countryside was pointless. We got to know some of the Greeks, one of whom was Averoff, a banker and one of the wealthiest men in Greece.

Another distinctive group in the camp was the "Americans", immigrant Jews who had been deported from the United States. These were a collection of hoodlums, second-story men, drug dealers, con artists, counterfeiters, racketeers, hold-up men and white-slavers. Some had achieved international reputations. One of them, Lieberman, was a renowned counterfeiter who let it be known he was willing to trade on his talents. He was later removed from the camp and sent to Germany to make fake U.S. and British currency.

Much of the day-to-day management of our lives in the camp was left largely to us. The camp administration gave us eight lira per day for food. We purchased our food in the magazinno. Everything was rationed, e.g., a quarter of a loaf of bread per day, one egg per week. We were able to make this go further by pooling our resources. A cook, also a prisoner, had been assigned to each barracks. We cooperated in making group decisions on the foods to be purchased and a schedule of meals. We occasionally received gifts from friends in Naples and every few months a package arrived from the Joint Distribution

Committee, an American Jewish overseas relief organization.

We also had another source of food — the peasants of the area. These people arrived at the barbed-wire fence almost daily with eggs, dairy products and vegetables. These foodstuffs had been withheld from the government requisitioners who paid them very little. Our fence became a lively black market. The guards looked away. Through careful planning, cooperative effort and trade with the peasants, we were able to assure that our meagre diet was nutritionally adequate.

As grain supplies fell off, a bakery was set up in our camp to bake an especially heavy corn bread. A prisoner from Pisticci, the camp for Communists, was brought to supervise the bakery. I became an assistant. This was very fortunate because this bread, when warm and fresh was delicious, but by the time it was distributed in the camp it became extremely hard and almost inedible. Each day I brought two fresh breads back to my comrades in the barracks where we delighted in its steamy fragrance.

Living under these conditions required an intense effort at cooperation. We had to organize ourselves to share the cramped quarters, to keep things clean, to arrange meals. Some of us received books from our friends outside and we set up a library in our barracks.

Life in the camp became organized and highly active because we had a great deal of time on our hands. We formed soccer teams, theatrical and choir groups. We had a cafe that served a delicious local wine that was black as shoe polish and was supplied by the peasants over the fence.

Even the "Americans" made their contribution to the social life of the camp. They organized gambling — cards, dice, chemin de fer and other games. The games went on most of the night, even though there were curfews. The guards received their bribes and looked the other way. However, there were frequent fights over the games and these fights held a threat for us, as they could have brought the camp administration down upon all of us with a heavy hand. Perhaps, this threat restrained the combatants who managed to avoid killing each other.

During these games large amounts of money appeared on the gaming tables. We knew that some people, including the "Americans" had brought money with them and continued to bring more in with the cooperation of the guards. They could afford to purchase a few luxuries for themselves and to play the games of chance.

What was the war for us? Where was the noise and violence? It was the occasional allied airplane overhead, obviously observing our camp. Mostly it was the newspapers, the radio broadcasts and the rumours the peasants brought to us. The guards let us read their newspapers and we listened to the one radio in the camp. We heard daily reports on the spectacular advances of the German Army into Russia — sometimes a hundred miles in one day. The guards were jubilant and they knew that the news had a depressing effect upon us, making us even more docile.

However, the reports of the one correspondent of the "Piccolo di Trieste" interested us and gave us many hours of speculation. He reported from the Russian Front in a surprisingly objective fashion, without the usual propagandistic flourishes. He described the desolated Russian villages and the battlefields strewn with Russian dead. We spent many hours trying to figure out what the correspondent was really saying. Was he an anti-Fascist sending hidden messages?

Then we began to pick up something else from the newspapers and radio. Even though the reports were optimistic, we sensed that the German army had been stopped in Russia and that the Italian Army had collapsed in North africa.

The tell-tale signs were close at hand. Every few weeks some of our Milizia guards were called up for a physical exam by the army. Our despised camp doctor was one of the first. Rumour told us that they were being sent into an Italian Division destined for the Russian Front. The German Army desperately needed help in Russia.

Our camp was not without its tragedies. My good friend, Griever, who hailed from a town near Cracow, finished a vigorous game of soccer and we found him in the barracks in a state of collapse. We struggled for hours to revive him, to no avail. The next day we buried him in a cemetery nearby. At the graveside we recited Kaddish, the Sanctification Prayer. Our prayer was interrupted by sounds coming from an old dilapidated tomb close by. I discovered the sounds came from a falcon's nest where three young falcons were setting. The mother falcon tried to chase us away. We held down the mother and took the two or three week old birds with us. The falcons became our pets and we raised them on the grasshoppers that abounded in our camp and with pieces of meat. We thought that they were domesticated, but one day they flew off, never to return.

A year later, we visited Griever's grave and found three more young falcons and took them back with us to the camp. This time we kept them longer and they seemed even more domesticated than the first group. As they grew up, they flew off for several days and then returned. One day they did not come back. However, several days later over 200 falcons roosted on the wires around our camp. They watched over us, hovered overhead and wandered around the camp for several days. We told ourselves that our pet birds had brought their friends back to show off their former home. Then the falcons disappeared and returned no more.

Six months after the opening of the camp, a group of about 200 women arrived. Among them was an attractive girl from Poland — Mala. She came to Italy from Poland in order to take a boat to Palestine and was stranded by the outbreak of the war. She had trained in child care and served as a nanny to the Commandant's children. This position gave her a great deal of freedom to move about the camp. She and I became attached to each other and we met in the evenings in the kitchen after supper. My comrades were discreet enough to permit us a great deal of privacy.

Mala was an intense Zionist, determined to complete her journey to Palestine and to participate in building a new Jewish life there. Her position in the Commandant's household was useful. On several occasions we were able to make special requests directly to the Commandant without going through the camp bureaucracy. For instance, we arranged to have a gravely ill comrade transferred to the hospital in Consenza.

Our relationship had its hazards. One day we discovered that Mala was pregnant. This camp was no place for infants and an abortion was performed by a colleague, a physician from Germany. He did the operation with limited equipment and the most important drug we had was sulfanilimide. The abortion was completed without complications.

Perhaps the most important and useful institution in the camp was the Farramonti Medical Association. It was centered in our barracks which was made up predominantly of doctors and medical students. We organized this association soon after our arrival in Ferramonte This was especially imporatant in the first year because the first camp doctor was not trusted.

Because my training included study and clinical work in tropical diseases, I took responsibility for problems of malaria. The swamps around us were breeding grounds for malaria-bearing mosquitoes. We obtained a supply of quinine and instructed people on its use, and treated those who fell victim to the affliction. Not everyone followed the instructions to take their quinine regularly and we had cases of malaria among inmates, guards and the construction workers. We were kept busy from time to time dealing with the outbreaks of chills and fevers that malaria brings on. Fortunately, the type of malaria in our camp was not a virulent type and we did not have fatalities from it.

We took turns providing emergency services, and sometimes performed surgery, such as an appendectomy. We set broken bones and treated the wounds that the "Americans" afflicted upon one another. At first, we kept our distance from the camp doctor. The second camp doctor was a different personality and we developed a cooperative relationship. He provided us with some medical equipment and drugs, because he realized that it was impossible for him to look after the medical needs of 2000 people by himself. Through him, we made contact with the head of the hospital in Cosenza, Professor Docimo, and were able to transfer gravely ill prisoners to that institution.

One day I did him a very special favour for one member of the militia. His name appeared on the list of those summoned for an army medical examination. It was rumoured that thoes called up were to be sent to the Russian Front. Naturally, neither he nor his colleagues in the militia wanted to go. He knew that if he could miss this call-up, he was not likely to be called again. He consulted with me and I injected him with 10 cc of milk. The injection of foreign protein into his body produced a high fever and he was excused from the medical exam and his name never appeared on a draft again.

Our medical group performed an important function in the camp. We treated people for many types of ailments, acted as a public health service that reminded people of the importance of hygiene in the crowded circumstances and, most important to us, we maintained our own skill and interest in medicine. We knew with certainty that our efforts did help most of our 2000 fellow prisoners to survive in reasonably good health.

The beginning of the end of my stay in Ferramonte began at a meeting with the Commandant. He had called together all of the doctors in the camp. A camp for British prisoners required a doctor, fully trained and licensed to practice in Italy. The appointment was to be approved by the British through the Swiss Embassy.

We were asked about our credentials. It turned out that I was the only one in the camp with an Italian licence, Esame Di stato. My name was passed to the Swiss Embassy and a month later, the approval came through. I was ordered to leave for Corropoli.

I left Ferramonte at the end of October 1942. On that last night, the Ferramonte Medical Association honoured me with a party. They used all of their ingenuity to put together a banquet. We made speeches, sang songs and drank lots of wine. Our feelings were quite mixed. We were sad to part for we had become good friends. I was unhappy to leave Mala. My friends were happy for me that I would be able to be a legitimate doctor, although still a prisoner. Some were even envious.

They presented me with a certificate, designed by an artist in the camp, and signed by all of the members. Written in German, it testified that I was a full-fledged member of the Ferramonte

Medical Association. I believe it was the only such certificate the Association ever produced!

In the next few years I was to confront the war in a very different way. I would experience the war of violence and danger. I would also meet many other people who would help me get through these perilous situations and I would also carry on as a doctor even in the most unusual conditions.

Through the war years, I lost many of my personal possessions. But the one that stayed with me was the certificate of membership in the Ferramonte Medical Association. I never considered disposing of it. It remains with me today, as a reminder of important friendships and associations.

Chapter 2

DISTANT SOUNDS OF WAR

The air raid sirens whined over Naples. Our train was just arriving at the station. There was shouting and scurrying everywhere.

"Take cover! The shelter is over there" was repeated over and over again. In my compartment, the two guards and the German soldiers, who did not know that I was a prisoner rushed to get off the train and into a shelter. They forgot and left me alone.

I found myself in the compartment by myself, and heard the Royal Air Force planes pass overhead. They passed over the railway station several times. No bombs were dropped, then all was quiet for a while. Finally, the all clear sounded.

My guards returned for me and the German soldiers came back for their baggage. For the first time in many months I had a period — about forty minutes — with no guards or fences around me. During this time I sat and waited, not knowing what to do with the opportunity.

Dr. Salim Diamand

We left Ferramonte early in the morning, I and two Carabinieri. We boarded a train and had to change in Potenza. One of the policemen, a Carrabinieri officer, had a family in this town, and so we stopped for a very pleasant meal. I was treated as a guest of the family. This was a special experience for me — to sit in a normal household with a normal family. My captors treated me as their guest and I was accorded the respect that Italians normally have for a doctor.

We then returned to our train where I sat in a compartment with my guards. Nothing in their behaviour indicated outwardly that I was a prisoner. We sat there just like three ordinary travellers.

Now, for the first time, I saw German soldiers. First, a few who joined us in our compartment; more soon who boarded the train at stops along the way. None were aware that they were sharing their journey with an enemy prisoner who was also a Jew.

The Naples Station was swarming with German soldiers, all wearing the green uniforms of the Afrika Korps. Naples was the port of embarcation for Rommel's army in North Africa. It was also a treatment centre for the wounded and a rest and recreation centre for battle weary German troops.

The sights in the Naples station confirmed some of the rumours that had passed through our prison camp at Ferramonte. By this time, October 1941, we knew that the Italian Army had collapsed in North Africa and that the Germans had taken over the campaign and succeeded in pushing the British back into Egypt. We also had heard that the Germans were advancing much more slowly into Russia and had not succeeded in capturing Moscow or Leningrad. We also knew that the British had defeated Italian Navy at sea. The air raid alarm at the Naples station also confirmed that the RAF were free to move through the Italian skies, having won air superiority over the Italian and German Air Forces. At this point, we thought that this could be a long and drawn out war that could go on for many years.

While I sat alone in the train, unattended by guards and looking out the window at an abandoned station, I thought of escape. No one could block my way now. But where would I go?

What would I do? Perhaps, my friends would help. But I knew that some had been conscripted into the Army and others were interned for security reasons. Who would risk their own security to help me? Perhaps, the habits of imprisonment and the prisoner mentality had affected me more deeply than I had thought. I sat in the compartment and waited for my captors to return from their shelter.

Our train continued across the Appenine Mountains that run down the middle of Italy to the eastern side of the peninsula, where the country slopes toward the Adriatic Sea. This was the Abruzzi region, a hilly mountainous area. Our train trip ended at Teramo and we proceeded by car to Coropolli, about 20 kilometers away.

The British camp was located in an old Abbey, outside the town. Although a prison camp, it was quite different from Ferramonte. There were a little more than 100 prisoners. The old, abandoned abbey was without any fences or visible barriers of any kind. This camp appeared to me to be more in the Italian tradition of exiling political and war prisoners to remote areas of the country without fencing them in. The remoteness and isolation of the place would help keep the prisoners in place.

In this camp, I had envisioned a group of fair-haired, fair skinned Anglo-Saxons and Celts, all speaking in the accents of the British Broadcasting Corporation. Instead, I found a melange of the entire British Empire, many kinds of accents, and some who could barely speak English. The one thing they had in common was that they were civilians who carried British passports. There were Greeks, Cypriots, Maltese and even Italians.

There were about a dozen Maltese whose families had moved to Libya when the Italians took control. In speech, mannerisms, appearance and food preferences, they seemed as Italian as any that I have ever seen. There was also a group of Yugoslavs who had been taken prisoner, who did not qualify as "British" in any way.

I am escorted into the Commandant's office. He greets me in a friendly fashion. "Soon you will meet Dottore Habibi", he tells me, "and he will show you what to do." "If you now have a doctor, why do you need me?" The Commandante leans forward with a confidential air and says, "Habibi is a trouble maker, and he will be transferred to another camp in a few days. Since you are not a British subject, we expect you to be more cooperative."

I was taken out to meet Mr. Pritchard, an Englishman and chief spokesman for the prisoners. Even though we were to live at very close quarters, he always remained aloof, "Mister" to me. He was very concerned to absorving the proper protocol in his relations with the Commandante and other Italian authorities. Dr. Habibi was at odds with him and Mr. Pritchard was very pleased to have him go.

Then I met Dr. Habibi. He was a man of astonishing competence, energy and charisma. He was not one to take life as a prisoner with resignation. Rather, he took his captors to task for every infringement of their rights under the Geneva Convention, governing treatment of Prisoners of War. He reminded his fellow prisoners of their rights, organized petitions, demonstrations, and he even organized a strike for better food, medical equipment and recreation.

The authorities agreed with the recommendation of the Commandante to move Dr. Habibi out of this minimum security camp, which was so close to the sea that sounds of naval battles could be heard at times, and to move him to a more secure and more remote place.

Habibi, a Cypriot who had been born in Lebanon, showed me around the camp. He gave me advice on dealing with fellow prisoners and with the camp administration. He understood that my status might make me hesitate to act with the same "hutzpa" or cheek. Habibi moved on after a few days but I did not know his destination.

I was now the "Official Doctor", appointed by the British Government through the Swiss Embassy, and approved by the Italian Government. Therefore, I received a stipend from the British Government as well as my prisoner's allowance. I also received packages from the British Red Cross, the same as the other prisoners, even though I was not British. In relative terms I was one of the most affluent prisoners in the group.

Despite my exalted status, I was still a prisoner and lived with twenty-five other people in one room, with makeshift furniture. My only private space was a small room where my supply of medicines and equipment were kept and where I also examined patients.

At this stage, the demands upon me for medical attention were minimal. The prisoners were in reasonably good health. My examinations were quite limited to checking them over, administering first aid and, if anything more serious developed, referring them to the local doctor in Coroppoli. The village doctor was cooperative and we developed a friendly relationship.

We were a very small camp, and, hence, there was little for us to do. We went into the village, escorted by a guard, several times a week to purchase food. This enabled us to speak with the local people and to learn about happenings in the world. Within three months of my arrival many things had changed. We knew that the German Army had retreated from Moscow and that the Americans had entered the war.

Our mood became bouyant and we spent a great deal of time talking about war and politics. We became experts on the execution of the war. One of the Maltese had a brother in the RAF, a celebrated hero. He reflected his brother's glory and put himself forward as a man with a detailed knowledge of tactics and strategy. Another Maltese, named Chiaruggi, who had been deported from Libya, was very impressed with American technology. He went on, obsessed, and described in detail for us a huge airplane the Americans possessed that had 24 engines. In spite of our laughter, he insisted he was correct.

One of our evening diversions was to organize seances to communicate with the spirits. Our contacts with the "other world" usually produced hilarious scenes. Whenever the lights went out someone would call "now escape". No one escaped despite the light security. In this area, on the eastern side of the Appenines, there were few towns and fewer roads that could lead to safety. The sea was close by, but we had no way to navigate it. In short, we had nowhere to go and no one to go to.

One of the projects that kept the camp busy for many months was the Serbian Zrinsky opera performed by the Yugoslavs. This group was comprised of mainly Tito supporters, with some monarchists and republicans. Their arguments were frequent, long and very noisy. Often it seemed that they would come to blows. One of them was a music professor from Fiume, the Slavic area around Trieste that the Italians had taken from the Austro-Hungarian Empire after World War I. He managed to pull them together into a choir and even got them to perform a traditional opera about patriots who oranized resistance to the Turks in the 15th and 16th Century.

While life was quiet for us at Corropolli, we still knew there was a war. At night we could hear the sounds of gunfire coming from the Adriatic Sea. The firing seemed so close, but we were told that it was really quite far off, just that the surface of the water carried the noises quickly and magnified this along the way. Nevertheless, as the months passed, the sounds of war that reached us at night began to come more often and we were certain that they were closer. We knew it might mean freedom but it could also mean great danger for us. We listened in the night — and waited.

Our captors also listened. They heard that the Germans were finished in North Africa and that the German Army was retreating all along the Russian Front. Our camp was now thought to be too close to the sea and we might become security risks. Therefore, we were ordered to move to a location about 45 kilometers inland, to a higher altitude on the Appenines.

Chapter 3

BEYOND THE "BAGNA ASCIUGA"

"They will not land on Italian soil and if they do, they will not get beyond the bagna asciuga", Mussolini promised in the Spring of 1943. "They might land at low tide," he said, "but they would all be immersed by high tide and never see dry land." This announcement came within days of our arrival at our new camp near Cillitella del Tronto.

There was a new mood around us. The Germans and Italians were surrendering in North Africa, the Germans had been defeated at Stalingrad and were retreating all along the Russian Front. Victory for the Allies and freedom for us was a matter of time. But time often seemed without end.

We were relocated at the abbey near Cillitella del Tronto. Unlike our previous camp, this was a church facility that was still used and, therefore, was in good condition. Daily services were held in the church that was attended by the local populace and the prisoners. This kept us in contact with the local people. The

Franciscan monk, who looked after the church, and I became good friends. I ate with him occasionally and we played chess.

Our buildings were located around a central square with a tall wooden cross in the centre. When we arrived the camp was already occupied by a group of people, deportees and refugees, from Germany, Libya, Tunisia, Poland and other parts of Europe. About two kilometers away, on a hilltop and separated from us by a ravine, was another group of prisoners — all Jews from Italy, Southern France and North Africa. They were housed in an old castle that had been abandoned for many years.

As in the camp at Corropolli, we had no fence around us and we were much closer to the village. The church, operating in our midst, brought us into constant contact with the local people. We were permitted to go into the village with a guard accompanying us. As our relationship with the guards was good, we spent a great deal of time in the village. We traded with the local people and a lively black market developed between us, while the guards looked the other way at all of this illegal trade. We obtained food beyond our rationed allotments and sometimes we secured things to make our lives a little more comfortable. We not only traded with them but also we spent a great deal of time socializing with them in the cafe. We heard rumours about partisan activity in the region but no one reported any partisan actions in the immediate area.

While the Italians had never been arrogant with us, they were always quite confident about a final victory for their country. However, now their elan was slowly melting and their manner became increasingly subdued. They now began doing something that was illegal for both them and us.

The village bar had a radio and when we came in they turned on the Italian broadcasts of the British Broadcasting Corporation. In the summer we listened with them to the announcements that Sicily had been invaded and then, in September, that the allies had landed in Calabria and Salerno. Then we heard that Mussolini had been deposed and replaced by Marshall Badoglio. An Armistice was signed by Italy. Then the Germans rescued Mussolini and installed him in Northern

Italy.

All was in flux. The German Army had taken over much of Italy, including Rome. The news and rumours swirled. We were hoping and expecting the arrival of the Allied Armies immediately. However, their advances were very slow and our moods often swung from high exhileration to great depression as the battle of Italy dragged on and on.

One day, sitting in the cafe, the regular BBC news broadcast ended with this: "Greetings to Aunt Giovanna, the pasta is ready and the spice in the sauce is very sharp. It has to be served hot. Please stand by for further recipes." From then on the news bulletins ended with cryptic messages of this sort. The frequency of these messages increased and sometimes they ran on for as much as twenty minutes. All this indicated increased activity by partisan groups. The villagers repeated rumours that they had heard but none of the reports indicated any partisan activity in our area.

These messages gave us something to think about. We tried to decode them and make sense of them. We attempted to identify the pantheon of pagan gods whose names appeared among the messages as well as the other literary and historical allusions that turned up. Then, there was a host of gibberish words that challenged us, "Iaraganella non canta". As much as we tried to make the most of the time, it was a time of anxious waiting.

In this camp I developed a new medical practice. Only one doctor served the entire area and the need was far greater than he could handle. Therefore, many of the local people came to me with their ailments, especially people from the more remote villages in the mountains. I was also permitted to visit sick people in the outlying areas, even as far as 30 kilometers away.

Drugs and medical supplies were severely limited and even the local doctor had little more available than I. I saw a number of cases of diabetes in children, a hopeless situation in that time and place. All of these children died.

I did the best I could. My prescriptions might include bed rest, certain types of food and herbs, and exercises. These trips into the mountain villages enabled me to see an Italy that few people, including Italians, ever saw. It was an area of great poverty and stoical people, determined to survive.

These were proud people who appreciated my ministrations. They insisted upon paying me, no matter what their poverty. However, they had no money and rarely saw cash. Besides, money had very little value now. They paid me in kind — chickens, sausages, salamis, cheeses and lots and lots of eggs. My trips into the mountain villages gave me the opportunity to receive the hospitality of these generous people.

I would return to our prison compound heavily laden and soon I possessed a larder of foodstuffs. I used these to trade with the guards and the villagers, who were experiencing difficulties with food. In the camp itself the British Red Cross parcels arrived less frequently and my supply helped us to keep eating satisfactorily. Because I had such a large supply of eggs, I requently made up a huge omelette into which we would dump the canned corned beef that came in our Red Cross packages.

The Allies had landed in Italy at Calabria and at Salerno. Immediately, there was a movement of people from the South into our area wanting to be away from the battles that would take place. Many Neapolitans came into our area looking for refuge. Then on September 8th the priest announced at the Mass that the Italian Government had signed an Armistice. Coming out of the church everyone was buzzing with the news. One Neapolitan coming out of the church proclaimed in his local dialect, "Mosiamo Tutti American!" Now we are Americans.

What will the Germans do, we asked? The answers began to come quickly. We heard. The Germans occupied Rome immediately, rescued Mussolini, and German soldiers were pouring into the country. The Allies were past the Bagna Asciuga and well entrenched on dry land but where were they for us? They were still far off and moving slowly.

Our Italian guards left us on our own and we were in the midst of friendly Italian people and so far, in this war, we had seen very little of the Germans. How would they treat us? We were concerned that they would send us "up north" to Germany, where conditions were much harsher, we believed. We had heard very little of the labour camps and the death camps and did not really understand how harsh it could be.

We waited and then there was an earthquake, a mild tremor and then we waited for the second one that usually follows.

Chapter 4

THE SECOND TREMOR

An earthquake is normally followed by a second tremor. Our second tremor came to us a few days later — but in a human form. "The Germans are here, they're coming!", people were shouting. They pointed to the hill overlooking us beyond the Jewish camp at the castle. We saw some Germans dismounting from a small vehicle. They looked in our direction and then got into their vehicle and began to drive toward us.

We immediately began running for cover. I ran into the vineyard. We heard them drive into our abbey area and before we knew what was happening they were firing. Then the firing stopped and we heard them drive off.

All was silence. At first we were afraid to come out. As I hid in the vineyard I could hear the cries: "Mamma mia, mamma mia, Madonna mia!". Then silence again. "Venite, veninte, come out", I heard someone say who was crouching in the vineyard. It was a woman known as La Gobba Maria, Maria the Hunchback.

"The Germans are gone", she assured us.

We came out of the bushes and vineyards. I saw someone being carried. "Aquilino Lhanno Amassato", I heard. "Aquilino has been killed.".

Aquilino was an Italian from Libya who had been interned because he held a British Passport. Several others had been wounded but not seriously. I attended to them using sulfanilamide as my main treatment.

We became very concerned and preoccupied about our wounded and their future. We did not want them to fall into the hands of the Germans. Therefore, we quickly approached some of the local people and they agreed to take our wounded into their homes and care for them. A good friend of mine was placed in the home of La Gobba Maria.

This was our first encounter with Germans. We waited for the next one.

Later in the afternoon a German Captain showed up accompanied by a driver. Politely, he asked us to assemble in the square. "I wish to apologize for the shooting this morning", he said. "You will understand that we did not know of the existence of this camp and when mny soldiers saw your group from on top of the hill, they were certain that you were Partisans because we have been attacked in the last few days", he explained.

Partisans! This was news to us because we had heard of guerilla activity in our district. We accepted his attempt to calm our fears for the moment. "Please carry on as you were, we will not bother you", he concluded and left.

We were not bothered for a while. Each day some German soldiers in a small truck or a command car came into the camp, looked around for a few minutes and then left. Now we were truly on our own for the Italian guards had departed. We looked after our own affairs and carried on much the same as before.

But it was not the same. Despite the disinterest displayed by the Germans, we were uneasy. The Germans among us, Jews and political exiles, who had spent time in pre-war concentration Camps were extremely pessimistic and were certain the Germans were planning something. As the days grew shorter, our moods became darker.

Every day we wènt to the village cafe to hear the news broadcasts. The Allies were advancing slowly but steadily. The British 8th Army was heading up the Adriatic Coast in our direction. Most ominous were the many cryptic messages to Partisans and spies that now filled up the airwaves. Now, again, we heard rumour of Partisan acivity in our district. We felt that the Germans would do something because of their own insecurity.

What should we do? Some of the prisoners went off to the mountain villages to hide out. But they returned in about ten days with reports that there was very little food to be found in these very remote places.

We talked a great deal about escape. How and to where? The mountains around us seemed difficult and impasssible. To the South were the battle-lines and the likelihood of coming up against the German Army. Northward was out of the question. The beautiful Adriatic confined us from the east.

With a great feeling of helplessness and fatalism, we waited. Meanwhile, we could feel other tremors under our feet.

Chapter 5

"YOU HAVE TO BUILD"

A truck with three soldiers sped into our camp and screeched to a halt in the square. A sergeant jumped out and ordered us to assemble immediately.

"Pack your belongings", he commanded. "We have to evacuate this place. Do it quickly because we do not have much time."

We packed everything that we could carry. I packed as much food as I could carry. By 9:00 a.m. we were loaded onto the truck and transported over to the Jewish camp on the hill at the other side of the ravine. We were separated out — British subjects in one group and all others, Jews and non-Jews, in the second group. The Germans had assembled many trucks, some parked under trees to avoid detection from the air. We too waited all day under the trees. As we waited the Germans treated us with politeness, adding "bitte" — please — to every order.

At about 6:00 p.m., as darkness descended, our group, the

non-British, was ordered to stand and mount the trucks. Now all of the politeness of our guards disappeared.

"Schnell, schnell", they snarled and pushed us towards the trucks.

Our convoy moved away from the castle. We found ourselves moving slowly through the night on rough back roads. This particular night seemed especially dark and cloudy.

"Which way are we heading", we asked in whispers. We peered into the dark for tell-tale signs on the landscape. After a while we figured out that we were headed south and the word passed around giving everyone some feeling of relief. Though we were going in the direction of the battle lines, we thought this preferable to going north.

Our journey in the dark was very slow and the soldiers were very tense. We were not permitted to talk. Frequently, the convoy stopped and there were whispered discussions among the soldiers. We heard some bits of their conversations and learned that they were fearful of land-mines and partisan actions. They sent patrols ahead on the road and sent out to search the brush beside the road. Stop and start, stop and start; we moved along these bumpy roads.

After midnight we came to a gate beyond which were buidings. It was too dark for us to discern where we were and what kind of place we were in. Our trucks stopped in front of a large building. We came off the trucks and were led into the building, to a very large, windowless room. The room was extremely hot. Exhausted, we fell asleep.

We were awakened at about 6:00 a.m. to find ourselves in an enormous brick-walled, brick-floored room. Heat emanated from the bricks all around us. What kind of a place is this? We soon learned that this was a former brick factory owned by Fratelli Testa, and this room had been a giant kiln. Though it had not been used as a brick factory for some years, considerable heat was stored here and the bricks continued to give off heat. It was uncomfortably warm, even on the coolest days. We soon found out we were near Castelfrentano.

We were taken to a large room in another building where

many other prisoners had assembled. This room included many people from all over Europe, especially East European and Balkan people.

The Commandant, an officer wearing the medical corps insignia, introduced himself and went on to tell us why we were here.

"This is a labor camp", he said, "and you will be treated as laborers. Whoever tries to escape, will be shot. You have to build".

We sat there mute but we could sense that this man could be mean.

"We also need a medicaal man. Who is a doctor here?"

I sat at the back without saying anything. Next to me a Pole named Leimi, was about to stand up and point to me. I grabbed him and whispered, "Sit down and keep quiet!".

Meanwhile another prisoner raised his hand and the sargeant announced, "This is Doctor Fischer, he will take care of the inmates."

Why did I not volunteer? I was suspicious of the Commandant and what he might ask me to do. I had also heard that prisoner doctors were being sent to forward medical stations to treat German wounded, a task that I did not relish.

The German prisoners among us took some relief from the fact that we were in the hands of the Army and not the SS or some other organization that they dreaded. They felt that, at least for the time being, we were safe as laborers.

On that first morning we were taken down the road about eight kilometers away. Then we were handed picks and shovels and told to dig. We wre creating wide, deep trenches. The soldiers took the trouble to explain to us that we were digging an anti-tank defence system, a technique they had learned from the Russians.

As we went about our work each day, an RAF airplane would circle over us very low several times. The planes were so low that we could make out the pilot's head in the cockpit. No bombs were dropped and we were not strafed. The pilot would observe for a while and then move on. We sensed that they knew we were prisoners and felt safe in this knowledge. However, our guards were not so sanguine. When the RAF hovered overhead, they usually stationed themselves on a wide perimeter around us, ready to take cover quickly.

As slave labourers we worked from dawn to dusk, returning every night to our quarters in the oven. Our food supply was erratic. Some days quite meagre, limited to a few slices of bread. At other times it could be plentiful. If the guards received a large quantity of food, they shared some with us. On several occasions the guards went out into the countryside to forage food for us. If they found an abandoned cow, they led it back and we would slaughter and cook it. We were very near the war front and the front line was getting closer each day. This made our supplies uncertain.

As I soon discovered, most of the guards were overage conscripts and some were very young, about 17 years old. Many of them were Volksdeutche, people from German communities in Eastern Europe and the Balkans. Some were "instant Germans", that is German decrees had made them into Germans. For instance, one of our guards was a Pole from the western part of Poland that had been annexed to Germany formally in 1939 and was therefore conscripted as a German citizen. Another one was a 17-year old whose German forbears had settled in Poland centuries earlier and was, therefore, decreed to be a German. Both were typically Polish and spoke poor German. Most of these guards had been conscripted hastily, given little military training and then sent to this part of Italy. They were on odd group who, at times, seemed more at home with the prisoners than with their fellow Germans, because we could speak their mother-tongues and understand their backgrounds.

The guards were a good-natured lot who often spent much of their free time with us. One of the Poles would bring us tobacco leaves. Another taught us how to fashion pipes out of bricks. Sometimes they brought us wine. They learned a great deal about us. We even got them to address those who had doctorates (in medicine, philosophy, etc.), as "Doktor".

One of our guards, an agreeable, 17-year old Alsacian, Schwartz, from Saarbruken, was especially impressed by the academic qualifications of many of the prisoners. As he watched us work, he would frequently exclaim: "Such workers, supervised by an ordinary person like me."

Once, when I muttered something about wanting to have a good smoke, as I had not had any cigarettes for some time, the young Alsacian said: "Warten sie, Herr Doktor". He returned with a package of cigarillos that he opened and then gave me a cigarello. The package was intended for his father, but he gave some to me.

We were very useful to our guards in another way. None of them could speak Italian and most of the prisoners could. Therefore, whenever they went into the town they took one or two of us with them to act as interpreters. Not only did we serve as interpreters, but they thought that we would be a shield against Partisan assassins. Because my Italian was very good, I was frequently chosen to accompany them into town. I sat with my guards in the cafes, and helped them make their purchases in the stores.

My role as interpreter was not always pleasant. The most horrifying occurred one evening when a very drunk, 50 year old soldier wakened me. "Wir gehen suchen Maedels — we are going to find some girls", he said. I walked with him into the village. We stopped in the cafe and he drank some more. Then with an unsteady walk he led me out of the cafe.

He went up to the first house we came to, the home of a school teacher. He knocked and a boy about eight or nine years old opened the door.

"Wo ist die Mamma", he asks, not bothering to use his interpreter.

The boy stood there wide-eyed and mute with fear. The soldier did not wait for an answer; he pushed past the child and entered. I followed behind him. We were in a large room with a bed at one end. A middle-aged woman sat up in the bed and she appeared to be sick.

"Tell this boy to get out of here", he ordered me.

Dr. Salim Diamand

"Listen, don't do this", I responded, "think of the boy, how upset he'll be, he'll cry and remember this all of his life".

My appeal to his nobler instincts brought an immediate response. He whipped out his gun and pointed it at the boy's head.

I looked at the fear-stricken boy and then at his mother, who was sitting on her bed, unable to utter a sound. Her eyes implored me to do something.

I began talking and kept on talking. I talked about the mortal sin he was bringing upon himself. I pointed out that the woman was not young and a fine soldier such as he could do much better elsewhere with a younger woman and without forcing anyone. I told him that she was sick; who knows what diseases he might come away with. The soldier stood there, gun in hand, quite agitated and annoyed with me.

"What is this to you, these aren't your people", he shouted to me.

I kept on talking. Sometimes, he pointed his gun at me but mostly it was aimed at the boy. I kept the words flowing, trying to find new ideas, and repeating what had been said before. After a while he calmed down and listened to me, almost hypnotized by my outpouring. I was sweating and my mouth became very dry but I was determined to prevent him from forcing himself on the woman or killing anyone. Finally he put his pistol back into its holster.

"Come on, we'll look somewhere else", he said with disgust and anger.

We wandered around the town for a while longer, still looking for "maedels". As the effects of the drinking wore off, he forgot his original purpose and forgot his anger with me. He did not remember anything that had happened earlier. But I remember how close I came to witnessing rape and murder and possibly being killed myself.

For the first time as a prisoner I had to worry about spies among us. One day, one of our guards, a Pole from Silesia, came up to me and spoke in Polish.

Here, Doktorzhe", take these socks", he said as he handed me

DOTTORE! INTERNMENT IN ITALY, 1940-1945

a small package. "I see that you have worn out your socks".

Then he looked around and whispered, "Be careful of what you say, there are spies around here, don't talk politics".

I heeded his advice and limited my conversation to non-controversial topics.

However, there was one Pole, a 17 year old named Marcinek from Cieszyn with whom I used to speak frankly. I advised him to desert at the first opportunity and turn himself over to the British. One day he also warned me. He took me aside and pointed to a prisoner named Singer. This man, in his 50s, had left Vienna when the Germans occupied Austria and went to Japan. When the Japanese entered the war, he was handed over to the Germans and now he was one of us in this labour batallion.

"Uwasaj...watch out for him, he is reporting everything you are saying."

Most of the guards by now knew I was a doctor, but the camp administration did not find out right away. However, Herr Singer could be counted on to bring them up to date. One day a sergeant came to me and asked, "Sind sie ein Arzt, sind sie nicht — are you a doctor or aren't you."

"Yes", I answered. I was promptly given a kit containing cotton, iodine, scissors, some sulfa and aspirins. My pick and shovel days were over and I was a camp doctor again.

The front lines were drawing closer. The sound of artillery firing was louder and heavier in the distance. The British were on the other side of the Sangro River a few kilometers to the south of us. There was a great deal of traffic, men and equipment all around us.

Everyone was quite nervous. The soldiers worried not only about the advancing British but also about the Partisans who were talked about and, so far, had never been seen. One day, I was walking along a road toward a worksite. I reached for a piece of bread in my pocket, as a soldier on a motorcycle approached. In a flash, he jumped off his motorcycle, drew his pistol and pointed it at me. He searched me and moved on. More and more we were facing soldiers with drawn pistols.

One day, they did not awaken us for work until trucks began

arriving at the brick factory. The trucks brought wounded soldiers who had been fighting to hold off the new British offensive, to prevent them from crossing the Sangro River. Our camp became a first aid station with the critical cases going on to the hospital in Chieti.

Our guards, who had no experience in combat, were wary of approaching the wounded or talking with them.

"Ach,es geht nicht gut", they muttered over and over again. "We are in flight".

Later, we were sent out to continue our work at the anti-tank ditches. As we worked, an RAF plane circled overhead. Our guards, more fearful than ever of an air attack, stood well away from us, the likely target.

We continued working into the early evening, as the fog moved in from the sea. The sounds of artillery were louder and closer. The atmosphere was extremely tense. We worried about what was to happen to us. Would the Germans abandon us in the middle of a battlefield? Would they take us northward? Would these nervous soldiers view us as a security risk and...

We did not dare think further. The tension was becoming unbearable.

Chapter 6

ESCAPE

"Raus, Raus!" the two soldiers shouted as they stopped their motorcycles in front of our work gang. "Take these prisoners back to the camp immediately and don't waste any time."

The Germans had obviously made some decisions about us. We had no idea what our fate might be. I turned to an Italian, a Tripoltanean who had been arrested because he had a British passport.

"Let's escape", I said.

"Yes", he agreed. "We can hide out for a few hours until the Germans retreat."

We knew this was certain because we had seen the artillery pulling back and constant RAF activity overhead.

In the confusion and darkness we were able to walk away from our work gang and the guards. We then began to look for a place to hide until the British arrived. This proved to be futile.

We found that every ditch, gulley, building and stand of trees already had German soldiers crowded into them. We had calculated wrongly. The Germans were not going to retreat so rapidly. They were preparing to make a stand here. Working on the ditches, we did not see the larger picture. We did our work too well, perhaps. We had helped prepare a defence and were only a small part of bulwark that extended across Italy and included Monte Cassino. This was the Sangro Line, about 15 or 20 kilometers deep, where the Germans intended to stop the advance of the Allies. They did stop them, indeed, for many months.

There was clearly no place for us to hide among these German troops.

The Tripoltanean shrugged his shoulders, spread his arms up and said, "I'm afraid, I'm afraid we have to go back to the camp".

Feeling defeated in my first attempt to escape since I had become a prisoner, I agreed. We walked back, depressed.

When we arrived at the gate, we were greeted with abuse.

"Where have you bastards been. What do you mean coming in like this". Then we were passed through the gate with kicks and punches and shoved into our waiting group.

While we waited, the artillery duel grew in volume and intensity. The night was lit up by the flashes of the firing guns. The guards were nervous and irritable as they counted our numbers.

Then they ordered us to our feet and shouted, "Vorwarts", and we began to move. Those who were slow to start moving were kicked and punched. The guards shouted constant abuse at us as we marched through the gate. Our direction was north.

We walked through the dark for six or seven hours, a forced march through hills, streams and mountain paths. We were never on any roads. This was hard on many of the prisoners. We stopped at intervals and then continued on.

Our guards, the good-natured fellows from Castelfrantano, became vicious bullies. They pummeled and kicked anyone who did not stop immediately when ordered, anyone who did not start fast enough, or anyone having difficulty keeping pace.

Finally, we came to a schoolhouse. They distributed us 50 to a room. After a few hours of sleep, we were roused and continued the march in daylight.

I could now see the whole group. We were over a thousand men assembled from the camps around Castelfrantano. Now we included a few British and American Prisoners of War. Our column stretched about a kilometer as we marched.

Our movements northward were tracked by the RAF who appeared overhead frequently. Our guards stayed close to us, certain that that way they would be safe from air attack. As our march proceeded, the Germans became more vicious. No longer content to use their fists and feet, they began to use the butts of their rifles. Some of the marchers now had cuts and bruise marks from the guards' ministrations. These guards were determined to get themselves out of the battle zone as quickly as possible and we believed they would not hesitate to sacrifice us, if need be. Their mood and method did not improve as we moved on.

The sounds of artillery were fading in the distance. The British were not advancing as fast as we had expected or hoped. We trudged through the day until we came to a village church where we spent the night. They fed us bread and cheese that they had taken from the local people. It was clear that the Germans had a carefully prepared plan to move us northward, moving us to churches and schools that had been emptied for us along the way.

As we began the next morning's march, the guards kept up their abuse. We talked about escape again and the first escape happened that morning. A few rows ahead of me, an Italian Jew from Milan marched. He was elderly, tall and straight. His long white beard made him a Biblical vision, a Prophet about to denounce the evil doers. He said little to anyone and shortly after we left the school, he made a sudden dash for the bushes beside our path. None of the guards saw him because they were too busy kicking and punching people.

We reached a large farm on the outskirts of the village of Tollo. We gathered straw and found ourselves a place to sleep in the barns. This place had been a camp for Partisans from Yugoslavia, most of whom had escaped into the countryside.

We were given a day of rest here before continuing on the march. We had to stay inside the barn most of the day and were permitted short periods out in the barnyard. The three days journey on foot had been very hard on many of our people. Many of us were nearly barefoot as our shoes were torn on the rough paths. Most of the prisoners used the opportunity to rest and sleep. They could not think any more about the march ahead of us and the final destination.

I was determined to find a way to escape and tried to assess our situation. Our group was guarded by a handful of soldiers and we were surrounded by hills on every side. Any attempt to get out meant a dash up steep slopes in full view.

Throughout the morning the camp was visited by young women. Whenever they showed up, the soldiers would leave their posts to chatter with them in their broken Italian. I also suspected that these visits were not as casual as they appeared. The girls, I became certain, were here to observe and gather whatever information they could for the Partisans. The comings and goings of these women would be important to any escape attempt. My worry was what I would do once I went over the hill. Where would I go? How would I avoid the German soldiers swarming over the whole countryside? To whom could I turn? Who could I trust?

About 10:30 an Italian carrying a bag came into the barnyard.

"Where is the sargeant?", he asked.

"Are you a barber?"

"Yes, I've come to shave the soldiers."

Is this a man I can trust? His appearance, his manner and his voice give me an intuitive answer. I could count on him. I can take the risk.

"Can you get me away from here? Can you help me?" I whisper.

He looks at me warily and asks, "What do you want?"

"I want to get out of here."

He looks at me for a few seconds and tells me, "Wait".

About an hour later the barber had finished shaving and cutting hair and he passed me again in the barnyard. He looked me over again.

"Be ready for three o'clock, over the hill there", he motioned with his head. "I'll get word to Count Luigi."

My problem would be to get up and over that hill without being seen. To assure that, the guards would need distractions. I turned to one of the women passing by.

"Signorina, could you come by here at three o'clock?"

"What for?"

"If you can, come here at three o'clock. I would like to talk to you.", I said in a tone that was both pleading and insistent.

She stared at me and did not answer.

"And please, can you bring your girlfriends?"

Again she did not answer. With a non-committal look on her face she turned and left.

I was uneasy about my decision to escape and felt I needed someone to go with me. With a second person in on the plan I thought that I would be less likely to waver and have cold feet. I looked for a partner and chose Sawazynski, a man who had been in the Polish Embassy staff.

"Dobrze, doktorzhe", he replied, "we'll go together".

I began to prepare. First, I slipped out to a truck and removed the medical kit — bandages, scissors, aspirins and sulfanilamide and a few other drugs.

At lunch I asked the man serving the food, a Jew from Triopli, for some extra food. He looked at me and immediately understood my intentions and returned quickly with some bread that I stuffed in my pockets.

For several hours I sat inside the barn waiting and thinking constantly. Two guards were stationed on each side of the large barn door and my first task would be to get past them. I was counting on the young women to provide the distraction. What if they did not show up? What would divert them?

A little before three o'clock my signorina and her blessed girlfriends came along and engaged the guards. Then good fortune gave us a second diversion.

Dr. Salim Diamand

In the distant sky to the north an RAF plane trailing smoke was sighted. The pilot took to his parachute. The guards and the girls moved to a better vantage point to watch the pilot float down gracefully. Meanwhile the barndoors were left unattended. I started to move.

"Sabarginsky, come!", I called.

"Doktorzhe, maybe later", he replied and sat unmoving and sad.

I was on the move and could not waver and ran as fast as I could out the barndoor and toward the hill, as the barber instructed me. The hill was short, steep and exposed to view. Another hazard was a hut at the top that quartered German soldiers. I had to hope that no one was there and if they were, that they would not see me. The hut stood there threatening and monstrous. I approached and nothing stirred. Now I was past it and over the hill. Out of breath, I fell and rolled a short way down the other side. Then I picked myself up and continued running as fast as I could. I dared not look behind but there were no sounds of alarm from the camp and no running feet behind me.

Finally, completely exhausted, I threw myself into a vegetable field and hid among the low-growing plants. I listened for voices for the sounds of heavy-soled soldiers' boots in pursuit of me. There was only silence.

Then I heard footsteps approaching stealthily. I was no longer able to run and clung to the ground as closely as I could. The footsteps came closer and then I realized that someone was standing over me. It was a peasant.

"Sh", he muttered with his index finger to his lips. Then he motioned me to follow him.

"Go in there", he said, pointing to the pig-pen.

"What is this?", I thought. "Do I look like a wild animal?".

"What do you want?", he asked, soothingly. "Are you hungry?".

He left and returned with figs and a piece of bread. I ate more out of nervousness than any real hunger. It had its effect and I felt calmer and more secure.

"Where is the barber?", I asked. "Who is going to help me?"

"Wait, the man will be here".

"How come he is not here?", I asked apprehensively.

I sat in the pigsty all afternoon until darkness started to fall. I worried that I would be missed and search parties would be out for me. Finally, a man about my age came up to me.

"Dottore, I'm sorry to make you wait", he apologized. "I had to rescue a British pilot whose plane had been shot down and he parachuted down."

This pilot had craeted a diversion that made it much easier for me to escape the camp.

"Come with me and don't be afraid", he said.

We walked a short way to a house. On the verandah were two bicycles. He gave one to me and took the other one for himself. Then we walked down a path and came to a road. When we turned into the road, I saw a terrifying sight. Tiger tanks were lined up on each side of the road and German soldiers were lounging on and beside them.

Mario, my guide, led me toward them and then into a narrow passageway between them in the middle of the road. We walked between the tanks, our shoulders almost touching them. Mario was very composed and kept up a stream of talk in Italian. It was a good thing that he did all of the talking for I was unable to put together a coherent sentence in any language and I put all of my efforts into looking casual. The German soldiers all around us sometimes nodded to us and we nodded in return. Most took no notice of us at all.

I do not know how many tanks were lined up on the road, nor the distance we travelled between them. Probably not many, but it seemed like an endless line. Finally, we were clear of them and out of the village. We rode our bicycles along the country road for a few kilometers.

I marvelled at Mario for his calm and composure. He had been through a busy, tension-filled day. He had rescued the British pilot and now was taking me to safety. He was full of energy and no problem seemed insurmountable to him.

We left the road and came to a farmhouse. Mario knocked and a man admitted us. Inside we saw a large fireplace full of large flames. Another man sat beside the fireplace.

"Buena sera", I said.

He did not reply and stared at me for a while.

A lady came in and asked me to sit down in a very pleasant manner. Mario and I sat for about three-quarters of an hour, no one saying anything.

Then the door opened. A tall man entered. He sat down at the table, took out his pistol, and put it on the table.

"Come here and sit at the table", he ordered.

I came to the table, and sat facing him and his pistol.

"I am Count Luigi", he said. "Now tell me who you are."

Count Luigi was the name that the barber in the camp had given me. He was an anti-Tito Serb who was head of the Partisan groups in the district. I spoke to him in both Italian and Polish. He listened and questioned me closely as I told him about myself. He knew a great deal about the camps in which I had been a prisoner and tested me on many details.

After more than an hour of grilling, he put his pistol away and said, "You cannot stay here, eat, then come with me. I will find you a place for the night."

The lady of the house broiled some sausages in the fireplace and served them to me with bread, macaroni and wine. This was the first substantial meal that I had had in weeks. I ate and then left with Mario.

We walked through the fields near the village until we came to a small house.

Mario knocked and a man opened the door.

"This is Dottore Diamand. He escaped from the Germans and will stay here with you tonight."

"Good, come in Dottore", the man said.

Mario bid me "arrividerci" and left.

I was in the house with two brothers. One talked with me and the other sat silently. He told me that they were active with the Partisans. He said that he knew that I was Jewish and must be kept out of the hands of the Germans.

They were about to arrange a place for me to sleep, when I became concerned. We were only a few kilometers from the village of Tollo where I had made my escape. It was likely that if the Germans set out to look for me, they would get here quickly. I decided to sleep outside.

I walked about 300 meters until I found a low lying shepherd's hut that blended in with the landscape. It was made up of branches and leaves. I crawled inside and slept very soundly.

Chapter 7

A DOCTOR ON THE RUN

The next morning, I was rested and calm. I could now think through my situation. I realized that although I had succeeded in escaping, my situation was perilous. I could easily be caught by the Germans. I had to change my appearance and have a new identity.

I went back to the farmhouse and borrowed some shaving equipment from the brothers. I looked at myself in the mirror and then proceeded to shave off my moustache. Then I removed a false, porcelain front tooth that I had acquired as a student. Now my appearance was altered considerably.

Now my problem was my identity card. I still had my old ID card from Naples that was somewhat torn and tattered. This carried my name as "Diamand". If seen by a German, this would identify me as non-Italian and arouse the suspicion that I was Jewish. Sooner or later I would have to show my ID. My solution: make another small tear in the ID. This altered the upright part of the letter "d" and my name read "Diamano", a genuine Italian name.

My Italian speech was no problem. I had acquired a near perfect Italian diction and command of idiomatic speech. I was familiar with Neopolitan and several other regional dialects. I was confident that I could convince any German soldier and most Italians that I was a native-born Neapolan.

I stayed with the brothers for another two days. We were now certain that the Germans were not searching for me, but it was dangerous for me to remain so close to Tollo. The brothers directed me to another place.

I went along a path for a few kilometers to a hamlet further up into the mountains. This was a place with a few houses and farm buildings. As soon as I arrived I was greeted with recognition.

"Bon Giorno, Dottore", people said to me.

I was dumbfounded bacause they knew who I was immediately.

"What do you mean? You know?", I sputtered.

"You are from Naples, no?," a man said. "Please look at my child."

The word had gotten around the district that a Jewish doctor had escaped from a German convoy. They were especially interested in my status as a doctor because they had not had a doctor in the area for some time.

I was led into a house to look at a child in bed. I had no stethoscope or other equipment to examine the child properly. But I diagnosed the condition as a bad cold and recommended bed rest and liguids. This gave the worried parents some assurance..

I went to another house where a woman complained of vaginal bleeding. There were no signs of a miscarriage and she did not seem seriously ill in other respects. I could only come to the conclusion that she was suffering from an unusually profuse menstrual overflow. My prescription was bed rest.

I stayed in this hamlet for four days, sleeping in a different house each night. During the day I saw more people who came from the local area with their ailments. Fortunately, none were too serious that they could not be treated with diet, and bed rest. More important was the reassurance that came from my authoritative status as a physician.

While I was in this hamlet, I was treated as an honoured guest and was amply fed. They fed me macaroni a la gitarra, pepperoni croquante, corn meal pies, corn pizza and a vino cotto that had the taste of vermouth. I began to regain some of the weight that I had lost in the previous months.

On the fourth night I was sent to sleep at the home of a young woman whose husband had fought in Yugoslavia, deserted the army and joined the partisans. Everyone thought it a "good idea" that I spend a night there.

In the morning I was fast asleep on a mattress of cornleaves when we heard the motorcycles coming into the hamlet. I had no time to escape or hide. The woman was very calm.

"Don't be afraid", she said.

"What do I do?", I asked in panic.

"Act natural", she replied.

She calmly poured water into a wash basin and proceeded to wash herself. I removed my shirt and went over to the basin to wash as well.

"Act natural", she repeated as she opened the upper half of the door to the house.

Soon we heard the footsteps of a soldier approaching. He walked to the door and looked in at the two of us and then walked away. We heard him walking around the house and then move on.

I went to the door and saw three motorcycles parked in the middle of the hamlet. The soldiers were talking. Then two of them walked around one more time and then all of them left.

After the Germans left the people gathered outside to discuss the visit. They were certain that this was a preliminary to something else. Perhaps, the Germans were about to round them up for a labour brigade. Or would it be a mass expulsion when the British advanced?

They felt they had to protect themselves and talked about hiding in the woods or armed resistance. We all knew that it was urgent that I get out of here quickly. In the middle of these discussions, a man entered the village asking for the Dottore. They did not know him and pretended ignorance at first. Then they decided that they could trust him, they introduced him to me.

"Dottore, my padrona, has been wounded by shrapnel. Maybe you can help her."

I was still wary of this man. Was it a trick to lure me into the hands of the Germans?

"I don't know you. I don't think I can go with you", I answered.

"We know the peasants and he can be trusted", one man said.

"We heard that a woman was wounded by English shrapnel", said another. "Some of us will go along with you."

I picked up my 'medical bag' and went with a small party down the road for a few kilometers. We were heading in the direction of the fighting. We could hear the sounds of artillery as we walked.

My companions decided to wait for me at a certain point while I went on with the peasant. They felt a group walking together in the area would attract the attention of Germans.

The peasant and I walked on until we came to his padrone's house, the home of a modestly affluent land owner. A tall elderly man came out to meet me with warm greetings. He led me to his wife. She was clearly older than he and I learned that it was the custom in the district for men to marry women older than themselves.

After washing my hands I examined the wounds. A ligament in the upper part of her right leg was torn by shrapnel but none of the shrapnel had lodged there. Eaerly signs of infection showed but there was no fever, a positive sign indicating that the infection had not spread. I cleaned the wound with hot water and hydrogen peroxide that they had in the house. Then I spread sulfa over the wound.

When I finished, the land-owner took out his billfold and began to take out a large number of bills.

"What am I going to do with money?", I laughed. "I cannot

buy anything with money around here."

"But I must pay you in some way", he hesitated.

"Well, I have companions and we need food", I responded.

He disappeared and returned with a basket of sausages, salami, bread, wine and cheese.

"Dottore, you don't need to go. I will send my helper and he will bring it to your companions".

I realized that it might be wiser not to return to the hamlet because of the visit by the Germans this morning. The peasant, knowing the lay of the land, would be able to deliver the basket to my companions without running into the Germans.

As we sat in the farmhouse, the artillery fire from the British side became heavier and was closer to us.

"We cannot stay here in the house", the landowner said. Carrying the padrona, we moved into the orchard. The landowner had prepared a grotto in advance and he had bedding and food dispersed among the fruit trees. As we settled in, the farmer left us and returned with as many bottles of wine as he could possibly carry.

Through the night the artillery boomed and some shells landed fairly close to us. We sat there and consumed five bottles of wine. The farmer told me about himself, that he had started life poor and acquired land. He had no children and he suggested that I remain with them, as he liked me.

It was dangerous for me to stay in one place too long and I moved on each day, staying in the homes of the more affluent farmers. Wherever I sent, people knew that I was a doctor and they sought me out. I treated their ailments as best I could.

I was now well-known among the Italians in the district and wherever I went people immediately identified me. While this helped to keep me reasonably well-fed and housed, I worried. I felt that the Germans would sooner or later find out where I was either by treachery or by accident.

Chapter 8

THE DOCTOR SEARCHES FOR A CURE

We spent our nights in the cave while the artillery roared outside. Each morning, when it was quiet, we came out to survey the
damage. The house was undamaged, though pock marks in the
earth indicated that some shells landed very close.

I stayed with the padrone for a few days. He liked me and
wanted me to remain there. But I was anxious about my situation
— I was after all a recently escaped prisoner. It was dangerous for
me to stay in one place too long, especially so close to Tollo, from
where I had made my escape.

Over the next few weeks, I wandered from place to place. The
peasants welcomed me as a doctor and as far as they knew, I was a
refugee from Naples. They asked me to attend their sick people
and I did the best I could for them under the circumstances.

They paid me with food. Most peasants had prepared for the
exigencies of war long before. They hid much of their produce
from the Italian Government requisitioners. When German

Dr. Salim Diamand

Army foragers visited them, the soldiers removed the food the peasants arranged for them to find. Satisfied, the soldiers searched no further and moved on.

I ate very well from the peasants' larders. But good eating took its toll on me. I had a nagging, persistent toothache and the aspirins I had at hand hadn't helped. I was told an Italian Army dentist was stationed in Villa Magna, to look after soldiers in the area.

When I arrived at Villa Magna, the dentist was no longer there, having departed when the Italians signed the armistice. What to do? The pain was unbearable. My distress showed as I stood there in front of the vacant dental office. Then a villager approached me.

"I'll pull your tooth", he offered.

I looked at him and hesitated.

"I can pull your tooth. I've done it for many people. Ask anyone around here."

"Okay", I said, ready to try anything. "Just bring this pain to an end. It's been going on for too long."

He took me to his home in the village.

"Sit down on the stool", he directed me. Then he poured some liquid from a bottle into a glass. "Drink this!"

It was grappa, a drink the peasants distill from local grapes. It tastes like congnac, but stronger. I swallowed the drink quickly and felt a numbing effect on all parts of my body except one — my aching tooth.

My "dentist" cut a length of string, made a loop, and ordered me to open my mouth. With deft fingers he slipped the string around my molar and yanked vigorously. The string slipped off the tooth. He tried again, again, and yet again.

The pain became more intense. I am going to die, I told myself.

"I don't understand it", my healer said in exasperation. "It's always worked before. Well I can't pull your tooth but I can do something about the pain."

I was unable to say or do anything to stop him and he went about heating a brick in the fireplace. Then he wrapped it in a piece of cloth, and put it to my face.

The immediate effect was to sting and burn my skin. But it worked. The aching diminished and then disappeared as I sat there through the evening with him and his two sons. For several days I wandered around with a scarf around my head. By keeping warm, I was able to reduce the pain.

The next day, the two sons and I walked down to a mill by the stream. Suddenly, we caught sight of two German soldiers walking along the other side. Quickly we went inside. They appeared to be on a routine patrol, not looking for anything in particular. When they cme to the mill dam, they crossed over to our side and walked in our direction.

"I'm afraid of what they will do if they find me here", I said to the two youths. I was not carrying any papers and if I could not produce the ID, I was certain to be arrested.

"Don't worry", said the older one. He walked over to the wall where two axes leaned, picked them up and handed one to his brother.

"Don't be afraid", he assured me. "There are two of them and two of us. If they try something, we'll kill them."

We waited silently as we heard the footsteps approaching. The soldiers came closer. They stopped in front of the mill house, exchanged a few words between them and then moved on. We waited inside the mill until they passed out of sight. The two brave young men went home and I remained there for the rest of the day not wanting to encounter the patrol while it was still in the village.

The next morning one of the villagers came to me. A very sick old man needed my help. I was led down the road and up the mountain side to a very lage grotto. A number of families took refuge here from the bombardment outside and lived here day and night.

The old man lay upon a mattress on the floor of the cave. I looked him over. All the apparent symptoms of heart disease were present. His ankles were swollen and he had frequent asthmatic attacks. What could I do for him? Very little! I tried to make him comfortable and could do little else.

Dr. Salim Diamand

I remained in the cave to look after the many children and adults who needed attention. Mostly people were suffering the effects of colds and mild influenza. Luckily we had plenty of aspirin among us.

Ferramonte Concentration Camp, 1941-1942 with its inmates, mostly Jews from Eastern Europe.

Ferramonte Concentration Camp, 1941-1942 with its inmates, mostly Jews from Eastern Europe.

Ferramonte Concentration Camp, 1941-1942
with its inmates, mostly Jews from Eastern
Europe.

Ferramonte Concentration Camp, 1941-1942
with its inmates, mostly Jews from Eastern
Europe.

Ferramonte Concentration Camp, 1941-1942 with its inmates, mostly Jews from Eastern Europe.

Ferramonte Concentration Camp, 1941-1942 with its inmates, mostly Jews from Eastern Europe.

Ferramonte Concentration Camp, 1941-1942
with its inmates, mostly Jews from Eastern
Europe.

Ferramonte Concentration Camp, 1941-1942 with its inmates, mostly Jews from Eastern Europe.

Ferramonte Concentration Camp, 1941-1942 with its inmates, mostly Jews from Eastern Europe.

Ferramonte Concentration Camp, 1941-1942 with its inmates, mostly Jews from Eastern Europe.

Ferramonte Concentration Camp, 1941-1942 with its inmates, mostly Jews from Eastern Europe.

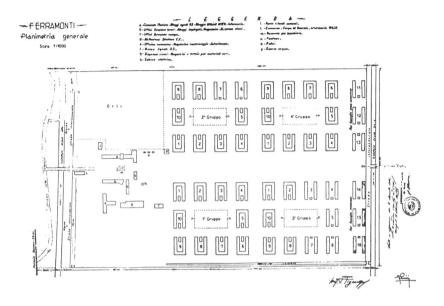

Ferramonte Concentration Camp, 1941-1942
with its inmates, mostly Jews from Eastern
Europe.

Ferramonte Concentration Camp, 1941-1942
with its inmates, mostly Jews from Eastern
Europe.

Ferramonte Concentration Camp, 1941-1942 with its inmates, mostly Jews from Eastern Europe.

Ferramonte Concentration Camp, 1941-1942 with its inmates, mostly Jews from Eastern Europe.

Ferramonte Concentration Camp, 1941-1942 with its inmates, mostly Jews from Eastern Europe.

Ferramonte Concentration Camp, 1941-1942 with its inmates, mostly Jews from Eastern Europe.

1940, Camp Campagna, Eboli.

1940, Camp Campagna, Eboli.

1940, Camp Campagna, Eboli.

1940, Camp Campagna, Eboli.

A gathering of friends in Naples, 1945, after the War.

Aspects of life at Camp Rivoli after the War,
1947-1948.

Aspects of life at Camp Rivoli after the War, 1947-1948.

Aspects of life at Camp Rivoli after the War, 1947-1948.

The Camp and Medical Staff at Trani.

The Camp and Medical Staff at Trani.

The Camp and Medical Staff at Trani.

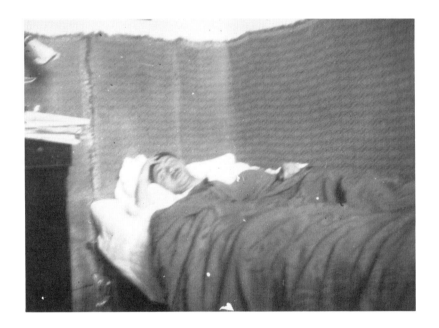

The Camp and Medical Staff at Trani.

The Camp and Medical Staff at Trani.

Chapter 9

HELP FOR A FRIEND

The grotto was virtually at the front line and refugees continued to arrive. Outside, the valley swarmed with German soldiers. At night and often in the daytime artillery thundered away.

A curfew was imposed after dark, under the penalty of immediate death. One evening as darkness was falling, shots rang out near our cave. We looked out and saw German soldiers firing at a man who was rushing to get back to the cave before nightfall. One of the bullets hit the man as he neared the entrance of the cave. He was dead by morning.

Everyone was horrified and a group of people went to the local commander to protest. He apologized and promised to reprimand the soldiers for shooting the man in the back. These gestures were made frequently by German officers to avoid antagonizing the populace. The delegation returned to the cave believing that the offending soldiers would be put into prison.

Dr. Salim Diamand

About a week later I was sitting in the crowded grotto when someone approached me.

"There's a man outside asking for the dottore", he said.

"What does he want", I asked.

"He says his father has been hit by shrapnel and he's running a fever".

"Do you know him?", I asked.

"No, he's a stranger. Comes from a contrada a way up the road."

"I don't think you should go", another man interjected. "It's almost dark outside and you'll get caught by the Germans for sure."

It could be a trick, I thought. We heard that the Germans paid rewards to those who turned in escaped prisoners. Everyone around me agreed that I should not go. Their advice and my fears prevailed.

"Tell him I can't come."

The man who brought the message went out to tell the stranger. I was afraid to identify myself to him.

The next morning I was approached again.

"Dottore, the man who was here last night is outside again", I was told. "He says that he is the man who helped you to escape from the camp in Tollo. His father is desperately ill."

I decided to take my chances and went out to meet the man. Immediately, we recognized each other. This was the man who had helped me escape the Germans.

"Mario", I shouted as I rushed to embrace him. "I didn't know it was you. I would have come last night."

"Well, I didn't know that you were the doctor living with these people", he exclaimed.

Secretly I was ashamed at having made him come again and present his offer — an offer that exposed him for his Partisan connections, a dangerous thing for him to do. For this brave man I would have done anything.

We set off and walked through the mountains, meadows and fields for more than an hour. Mario knew his way and we managed to avoid any contact with the German soldiers swarming in the district. He led me to a farmhouse, to his father, a man in his early 50s.

I examined him. He had a very high fever. His foot was very swollen. The wound on the instep was slightly bluish and discoloured and secreted a brownish pus-like material. As I bent close to the foot and pressed slightly I heard a hissing sound.

What is this? Then I realized that I was looking at a condition that all doctors learn of as medical students and few ever see in a lifetime of practice. My diagnosis was gangrena gassosa or gaseous gangrene.

"I can't do anything for him", I told Mario. "You must get him to the hospital in Chietti. Do you know any of the Germans?"

"Yes, I know the commander here".

"Then go to him and tell him about your father. Maybe, he'll send your father to the hospital in a truck. If you can get your father to the hospital soon, he might have a chance of surviving."

Mario thanked me. Both father and son kissed me as I left. Mario immediately set off to see the German commander and I walked back to my cave with another man.

As I went back I thought of Mario's father, who understood the gravity of his situation and bore up to it with fortitude. I could see where Mario had learned his competence and bravery.

Chapter 10

CLOSE CALLS

There was a lull in the battle for a few days but we could see a great deal happening. German soldiers, vehicles and equipment moved up and down the road constantly. Royal Air Force planes circled overhead, observing. Our constant concern was to avoid contact with the Germans.

Once a peasant came to me with a piece of paper.

"The Germans took my mule", he complained. "At least they gave me a receipt and maybe they'll pay me for it."

He showed me the paper and I read it

"Dieser Esel gehert uns (signed) Buns", it read. (This donkey belongs to us.)

He did not wait for me to translate and rushed off with his "receipt" to whatever satisfaction the Germans might give him.

My tooth continued to trouble me from time to time and this meant going about wearing the scarf around my head. It gave me some relief and almost brought disaster.

Dr. Salim Diamand

One day I went out with several others to bake some bread. We went down into the valley, crossed the stream and stopped in a vacant house to eat. An RAF plane passed overhead, followed by an anti-aircraft barrage. The plane was hit and the pilot parachuted down, not too far from us.

We knew that hundreds of German soldiers would be in the area in a matter of minutes and we decided to get moving. As we started to cross the stream, we met a German patrol, four soldiers, rushing to get across to the downed pilot.

They were passing us when one of them looked at me with my face almost covered by the scarf. He stopped.

"Look at this Italian's face", he said, pointing at me. "Why is that thing around his head. I don't like this."

While pretending not to understand German, I was very anxious for I had no ID on me. They would have arrested me for certain and my companions as well.

"Leave him alone and let's go!", said another soldier.

They argued for a few minutes and then decided to go on without checking us.

The next day we learned that German soldiers looking for the pilot had been attacked by Partisans. We now feared that there might be a round-up of men among the people living in the caves. Therefore, several young men and I decided to move out.

We crossed the valley and went up the other slope. We found a farmhouse and the farmer welcomed us in. He knew something about us from the group in our cave. He warmed up some fried chicken and the smell stirred hunger pangs in our stomaches.

"Don't expect to eat too soon", he advised. "The Germans will smell it too and should be here soon.

No sooner said than a half dozen German soldiers appeared. They walked, looked at us, and sat down to eat without a word. They ate all the soffrito — fried chicken with pepperoni, drank all the wine in the kitchen. They ate everything edible in the kitchen.

They looked like a disheartened lot who knew the war was lost. As they completed their meal they looked at us, nervously, as if worried that we might be Partisans. As soon as they finished, they departed quickly.

We, who were expecting a tasty meal, were unhappy at seeing all of this food disappear. The farmer smiled at us and vanished for a few minutes and returned with more chicken, pepperoni, bread, and wine from his secret storehouse.

"This happens almost every day", he explained. "As long as they leave with full stomaches, they don't bother me for anything more."

He fried up another meal for us. We stayed here another day and having learned that there was no round-up of people by the Germans, we returned to our grotto.

I remained in this cave for weeks, venturing out cautiously. The sounds of shooting reverberated through the valley day and night. After dark the fearsome artillery duels shook the earth and night skies lit up with the flashing of the cannon fire.

In the daytime we went out cautiously, if we had to. We never knew when the next artillery barrages might start up, or when an aerial bombardment might not come raining down upon us.

German soldiers, fearful of Partisans, were unpredictable when they became suspicious of civilians. Often they shot first and asked questions later. It was a time of hiding and fear and we were uneasy as to how the Germans might deal with us.

Chapter 11

IN THE FRONT LINES

The day before Christmas 1943, five German soldiers rushed into our Grotto in the late morning. They picked out a dozen men, including me.

"Come with us", they ordered.

We followed them down the valley to some farm buildings where lumber was piled up. They lined us up and piled bundles of boards on each of us and then ordered us to move on.

Under the watchful eye of our guards, we started to climb a small mountain. The mountain was frequently steep and we had to take a long circuitous route. The soldiers, determined to get to the top quickly, gave us little rest along the way

At one point, an RAF plane flew overhead, then circled around. Expecting bombs, I immediately dropped my load and jumped into a rut. The airplane passed without taking any action against us.

"Look at this Italian", shouted one of the soldiers. "Look how frightened he is. They're all like that."

He and the other soldiers laughed as they watched me get up dirty and dusty. Then the sergeant came along.

"Idiots", he snarled. "This Italian is the only smart one around here. When the English planes come over, you take cover. Learn from him."

The laughter stopped and we ascended the mountain. At the top the Germans had an observation post. They needed the boards to improve the shelter and earthworks.

We had a few minutes of rest when the captain came out and looked at us.

"A fine looking bunch of Italians!", he exclaimed and then turned to two soldiers and said, "Take two of them and get the mail."

Another Italian and I were picked and we went back down the mountain with the two soldiers. We walked through the woods and across several small streams until we arrived at an encampment in some dilapidated houses.

I worried as I watched the Germans here, fearful that one of them might recognize me, perhaps a guard from Castelfrantano.

The soldiers picked up the two sacks of mail and loaded them onto the Italian and me. Then we started to cross the valley and head up the mountain. There was one stretch of valley which was very exposed. Shortly after we entered this open portion, British artillery spotters sighted us and their guns opened fire.

They had us well located and bracketed. The shells landed very close — in front of us, behind us. We jumped into a hole and waited. When the barrage stopped we got up carrying our bags and walked on. Immediately another barrage of shells rained down on us and again we took cover in another hole.

We learned quickly. As soon as the firing stopped, we picked ourselves up even faster and started moving while the swirling dust concealed us. Then as soon as the dust settled we were ready for the next round of firing and took cover even sooner.

This was frightening and eerie. We saw no British spotters nor their guns, but they knew where we were all the time. There was black humour in the thought that I might be killed by the British

— my allies!

We kept moving across the valley, from hole to hole, in the gun-sights of the British 8th Army. At last we reached the sheltered slope of the mountain. We went up the steep mountain with our loads over our shoulders. The soldiers no longer felt a need to rush us along for they were glad to be alive. We finally reached the top where the mail was taken from us. We collapsed on the ground in exhaustion.

The soldiers gave us some candles and cigarellos that came with their mail. The captain came out, saw us and called the soldiers who accompanied us.

"How did they behave?", he asked, pointing at us.

"Herr Haputmann, they are brave Italians", the soldiers answered. "They behaved as good soldiers under fire".

They described our journey through the valley and emphasized that we never let go of the mail sacks. The captain called to the sergeant.

"These men are excused from all further work", he ordered loud enough for all of the soldiers. "They're excused and don't take them for any more work groups."

A German soldier accompanied us back to our grotto. As no shooting was expected on Christmas, many of the people had gone back to their homes for the holiday. One man invited us to his home further up the mountain side, above the tree line. More climbing and when we arrived, I collapsed and fell into a deep sleep.

A loud knocking on the door broke my sleep a few hours later. Two soldiers entered, soldiers I recognized from the observation post. One of them pointed at me and two other men.

"Come with us and move quickly!", he barked at us.

"But the captain said no more work for me", I protested, feigning a broken German.

"Come and don't give me any arguments", he ordered.

We went out into the night with the two soldiers, down the mountain side. The route was one that required us to walk in a mountain stream, ankle deep in cold water. Our shoes were worn, torn and soaked through.

Dr. Salim Diamand

They brought us to a contrada. One of the buldings in the hamlet was an army kitchen. We held large pots while the cook ladled soup, meat and potatoes into them. Holding a ear in each hand, we formed a chain to return up the mountain to the observation post. Now the rain started.

Again we walked through a shallow stream which passed through woods, thus shielding us from the British spotters. As we went up the mountain in the cold December rain, we almost dropped the pots a few times. The soldiers were abusive and threatened to shoot us if we spilled any food. A miserable journey!

Feeling extremely tired, I tried to get out of these duties by pretending to collapse at one point.

"What's the matter", a soldier asked.

I pointed to my ankle. His response was to curse. Then he took hold of my arm and pulled me to my feet. He grabbed the ear of the pot from my hand and carried it himself.

"Marshieren sie", he ordered.

I walked on with them pretending to limp all the way. Finally, we arrived at the post. The captain saw me hobbling in and he went over to the soldier who had pressed me into service.

"Dummkopf", he shouted. "Didn't I tell you that this Italian is excused from work."

"Aber, Herr Hauptmann...", he responded meekly.

"No buts", he shouted still louder. "This Italian did more work this afternoon than you've done in your whole life and he is a lot braver than you'll ever be."

He then proceeded to give the soldier "a dressing down" in front of everyone. He muttered curses in a German dialect that I did not fully understand. The soldier stood silent, his face changing colours.

Another soldier brought me some soup and a plate of meat with potatoes. When I finished, I went over to the stream to bathe my "injured" foot. The captain was solicitous and ordered a soldier to accompany us back to the farmhouse.

We were soaking wet and removed our clothes, placing them in front of the fireplace. Again I fell into a deep sleep.

At about nine o'clock, we heard some movement around the house.

"The Germans are here again", people whispered.

I quickly took a syringe from my pack and sterilized it with alcohol. Holding my right ankle tightly, I jabbed the needle, withdrawing some blood and then injected the blood under the skin in the other foot. Immediately, there was a swelling.

This time the German press gang was a large group which included a medical orderly.

The officer looked at the ankle and asked me to explain. There was a note of suspicion in his voice.

I told him of all I had done the day before and that I had sprained my ankle carrying food to the observation post. He called the medical orderly over to look at my foot.

"No, this Italian can't work", he said.

The Germans took their conscripts and left me behind with the women, children, the old and a few other young men.

The next day we learned that the group was taken to build earthworks for an anti-aircraft position nearby. The Royal Air Force bombed the site and all were killed.

Chapter 12

TOMASO AND HIS FAMILY

A few days after New Year's Eve, 1944, three German soldiers showed up at our farmhouse. They selected me and two other young men and ordered us to remove the old barn doors. One door was loaded on my back and I was told to start moving. It was very heavy, and clumsy to handle. I moved along like a human donkey.

The soldiers amused themselves as they walked behind me. They threw stones at the door as I stumbled along the mountain path. Each time a stone hit against the door, a tremor went through my body and I could feel myself weakening. A sergeant came toward us from the opposite direction. When he saw the situation, he shouted and swore at the soldiers because they had been ordered not to bring any Italian bearers with them. He ordered them to take the doors from us and sent us on our way.

The farmhouse seemed too easy a place for the Germans to find me. So I returned to the grotto. More people had taken refuge there. Many were old and sick. Mostly they were women for the young men and had been pressed into labour duties by the Germans or were in hiding elsewhere. We were crowded along the walls deep into the cavern. People sat by their oil lamps, the only source of light in the darkness of the grotto. The effect was haunting and eerie as the women sang religious songs — the words 'Maria tu Santi' were heard over and over again. At times they uttered strange sounding incantations in an unfamiliar dialect and engaged in magical gestures and rituals. I felt I was thrown back into very ancient times, possibly pagan times, and certainly not times and rituals sanctioned by the Church.

The younger people watched these activities and amused themselves by mimicking their elders. All of us were equally frightened as the sounds of fighting were heard in the deepest recesses of our grotto. Now we not only heard artillery barrages, but rifle fire, grenades, and machine guns. Occasionally, a sulphur-bearing breeze wafted into our cave.

One day, near the end of January, two German soldiers came to the entrance of the grotto.

"Raus", they shouted. "Get out! You can't stay here any longer. All Italians have to leave the district."

The people moved slowly; the infirm were supported or carried by their families. The soldiers were impatient with everyone and did not want to hear our problems.

I helped some old and sick people to their feet and was the last one out. As I emerged, a soldier recognized me. He had been the one who had selected me to carry the barn door and then tormented me with stones.

"That fellow got me into trouble with the sergeant", he said pointing at me. "I had to carry a heavy door because of him. I am going to shoot him."

"What for?", asked the second soldier, "You know that he didn't do anything to you, really, gehen, sie, let him go!".

They sent us along in the same direction as the others who were now out of sight. I never did catch up with them. Instead, I met a family — a husband, wife, a 16-year old girl, a seven year old boy and a small dog. Each of them were fully loaded with bags. They greeted me warmly.

"Where are you going?", I asked.

"We live in Contrada Ruscita. The Germans ordered us to leave the region but we're not going because we want to return home as soon as the fighting passes. What about you?"

"I'm a doctor from Naples", I answered. "The Germans just ordered me out of the region, too."

"Why don't you stay with us, Dottore. I know the district very well as I have lived here all my life. We'll survive."

So, I joined this family. The man was Tomaso Di Bartolmeo. He owned a large vineyard in Pergolato, in which he grew pergolato grapes.

We walked all afternoon. Tomaso knew everything about the area, what lay beyond every hill and who owned what farm. At about five o'clock we stopped in a narrow valley between two hills. We unloaded the bags. Tomaso removed a hunting knife and proceeded to dig into the sandstone rock at ground level. He created five niches in the rock large enough for us to sit in. He wanted to protect us from the shell-fire that would be coming down around us at nightfall. As he finished each niche, we had to sit in it to try it out for size. He was meticulous about his work, like a tailor fitting a customer.

The Tomaso family carried a lot of food and that evening we had bread, salami and grape marmalade. Then we settled into the niches and tried to sleep in a sitting position. As I nestled myself into the hillside niche, I could not help but compare our positions to the statues of Saints that occupied niches in the churches.

The artillery roared all around us and shells exploded close by. We were well protected between the two hills and no shells fell into our valley. I managed to fall asleep.

In the morning we woke to a bright sunny day. Things were much quieter and the sounds of firing were very distant. We came out of our niches to eat breakfast.

Tomaso was very quiet and looked quite distracted, as if he were trying to hear something in the distance.

"What's the matter?", I asked. "Are you not feeling well?"

He did not seem to hear me and sat silently as if listening for something. Finally, he broke his silence.

"I...I can hear my sister's voice", he said softly. "I think she says the Germans are gone and the English are here."

He sat for a few minutes longer, absorbed in the voice he was hearing. Then he stood up and spoke.

"Wait here. I am going up". He went up on one of the hills, looked around and called to us.

"I am sure my sister is going to the well for water. I can hear her voice. I recognize it. I am going to find out what happened."
He left.

We waited several hours, unsure of what was happening. We remained where we were. We knew that the Germans did not want any Italians in the district and we did not want to take any chances on getting caught. Eventually, Tomaso returned, looking sad and dejected.

"The Germans are still here", he announced. "They held off the English attack. It looks like they'll be here for a long time."

This news depressed us for we had been expecting Tomaso to return with a different story. Now Tomaso proposed that we move on to a safer place. We left our valley and entered a landscape empty of people. We passed through abandoned villages, hamlets, by buildings that should have been full of the sounds of people. Instead, we saw no human faces nor heard any voices other than our own. We followed Tomaso's route and we met no Germans along the way.

We climbed up a winding mountain path until we came to the narrow opening of a grotto. The entrance was about five feet high but inside we found ourselves in a huge sandstone chamber, about 30 feet high. There was straw on the floor, left by shepherds who had used the cave as a refuge against the weather. We remained here quietly for a few days, listening to the sounds of gunfire in the distance and not going very far from the grotto. The cave was fairly high up on the hillside and seemed fairly safe from any intrusion by the Germans.

Then our food supply ran out. Tomaso decided to go out to forage.

"Most of the farms are abandoned", he explained, "and I know where the peasants hide their food supplies."

He left us and we waited for several hours, becoming more anxious about him. Finally, he returned with salted bacon, cornmeal, wine, and some pots and pans. We had no matches but Tomaso had found some sulphur.

Outside the entrance, he put the sulphur on a rock and rubbed it with a wire. Soon he produced a spark that lit the straw and in no time we had a small cooking fire going. It had to be a small fire; otherwise, it might attract the Germans. As we ate, I admired Tomaso's resourcefulness and knew that with him around we could survive almost anything.

The next day, he took me along with him, leaving his family in the grotto. We walked down into the valley until we came to an abandoned house.

"This place belongs to a friend of mine", he said, "and he won't mind if I help myself to some of his food. Actually, they are all friends of mine."

He went straight to a hidden door and we helped oureslves to some of the food in the secret larder. Then we went on to another place, owned by a local vintner. It was a house and winery combined. A large vat was on top of the building. The Germans had been here before us and had sprayed the vat with bullets. They obviously suspected that Partisans were hiding in the vat. The wine from the vat had seeped into the house below. When we entered the house we stepped ankle deep into white wine. The vintner, being more prosperous than others, left behind a supply of fine meats and other foods. We loaded our bags and departed.

We went out to forage each day. No Italians remained in the area as far as we could see and we never encountered German patrols. However, we knew that the Germans observed us. The valley was dominated by a small castle, La Torre della Muchia, which the Germans occupied. The tower built in Napoleonic times had been the local administrative centre during the French occupation of this part of Italy before Unification. We assumed that the Germans were not bothered by our presence — at least not for a while.

Living off the larders of abandoned farms, we satisfied ourselves on food and wine. Only one thing was lacking — tobacco. And I had a desperate craving for cigarettes. In our desperation, we smoked grape leaves and they were not too bad. One day it was raining and all the leaves were wet. So I tried some straw wrapped in paper. The vile taste in my mouth ended my craving for tobacco for many months.

When we looked down into the vallley or wandered down, we found not a single sign of life. However, one night we were confronted by a German soldier. He knocked on the door of the grotto.

"Was machen sie hier", they demanded and then in broken Italian, "what are you doing here, you're not supposed to be here."

"We're working for the German Army and they let us stay", I answered.

"That may be so", a soldier said, "but I have my orders and you have to go. If you want to stay here, you'll have to go to Pescara to get a permit from the commander. We'll let you stay until tomorrow. If you don't have a permit by tomorrow, you'll have to go."

They left and we went back to bed. We did not go as ordered because Tomaso was determined to stay close to his home.

Within a few days the sounds of firing came closer and one day we observed from our grotto that two soldiers left the castle, came down into the valley, crossed over and came up to the path leading up to our cave. They lined us up, searched the cave and told us firmly that we had to go. This time they accompanied us to a contrada where they had rounded up 40 or 50 other people who had remained behind. We were loaded onto trucks and taken to another place by the sea where we waited for food. We stretched ourselves on the beach but as soon as we made ourselves comfortable, the British Artillery opened up on us. Shells rained down, falling into the water and on the beach. We ran to the trucks and were moved further up the road to a more sheltered spot.

We were given food. While we ate, I struck up a conversation with an Austrian Corporal, a school teacher.

"Where are you from?", he asked.

"We escaped from Naples", I answered.

He looked at me knowingly, obviously assuming that we were fleeing the Americans at Naples. He naturally thought we were Fascists, or Nazi collaborators.

"Don't be afraid, if you go north", he advised "People like you can find work with the Todt Organization." I later learned that Todte was a construction company that employed slave labour throughout Europe.

He took out his billfold and removed 2000 Lire. "This is for the five of you", he said and proceeded to distribute 400 Lire to each of us. This was an empty gesture as neither he nor we could use the money anywhere around here.

As soon as it was dark, we mounted the trucks and travelled north a few kilometers. We were quartered in a barn where the Germans stored cases of beer. I looked at the cases and announced that I was going to have some beer.

"The Germans will kill you!", Tomaso said. I could not resist and took three bottles out. Luckily there were empties in the cases and my empties were not the only ones to give me away.

The next morning the Germans told us that they had work for us. They sent us out to work on the roads in howling rain and snow. In return we were given food.

The next day we were sent out to saw logs. On the way back to the barn, I saw a pair of boots, German boots soaked in blood. A German soldier saw me looking at the boots and then noticed my worn shoes which now exposed my toes.

"You want them?", the soldier asked. I nodded. "Then take them but don't dare sell them or you'll be shot. Understand?". I agreed.

The boots turned out to be too small for my feet but in desperation I squeezed my feet into them and then walked uncomfortably down the road. After a while I realized that I would not be able to wear them. Luck was with me. I met an

Italian boy leading a mule. He was wearing a pair of German Air Force boots, much too big for him. We looked at each other, passed a few words, and agreed to exchange boots. Both of us now had nearly perfect fitting footwear.

The next day there was little for us to do. The soldiers had been drinking beer and decided to set up a firing range, using the empty bottles as targets. They selected me to set up the bottles and to stay down range to set up bottles after each firing. Some of the soldiers were quite drunk and I worried about my safety.

When they finished they took me to drink with them. I entertained them with sentimental Neapolitan songs. My reward came the next morning when I was told that the Di Bartolomeo family and I could leave for Chietti. They also gave us two bicycles. Tomaso and I took the bicycles and went ahead to look things over in Chietti. As we started Tomaso looked unhappy. After we had cycled a short distance, we stopped.

"I don't want to go to Chietti", he said. "There's nothing there for me. I want to stay here and get back to my village as soon as possible."

"I have to get away from here", I responded. "I might be able to find someone to help me in Chietti." Tomaso nodded gravely. He knew intuitively that I was running away from something, though he knew little of my past history.

We returned to the German camp and spent the evening together saying our farewells. The Di Bartolomeo family had become my family and I was like an uncle to the children. I admired Tomaso for his endless resourcefulness and his iron will to survive. It was a sad parting.

The next morning I walked into Chietti.

Chapter 13
_____

A HELP AT THE GESTAPO

I walked into Chietti one morning in February 1944. This was the first time that I had walked in the streets of a city since I was arrested in June, 1940. Chietti was full of refugees and German soldiers. I was struck by the appearance of these soldiers, so different from those I had seen in the last few months. These men were neat, clean-shaven and often in dress uniform. They strolled about the streets and sat leisurely in the cafes. Their appearance hardly suggested an army in retreat and they looked as if they were here for a long stay.

The effect on me was depressing. I had survived until now but I felt sorry for myself because I was now among an army of German soldiers. I walked along buried in dark thoughts. As I passed an archway leading to an apartment courtyard, I did not notice a man lurking there.

"Dottore", the man called softly. "What are you doing here." I turned to the man and recognized him as someone from

Dr. Salim Diamand

Feramante, the concentration camp.

"Jacobson, what are you doing here?", I said as I joined him in the archway.

Jacobson was a man in his 50s. He told me that he had escaped from Feramante. One of the few who did successfuly. However, he had landed behind German lines, while everyone who had remained in Feramante was now liberated by the Allies.

"I went to the Gestapo and convinced them that I was a Latvian, who had fought the Bolsheviks in 1918. They believed me and I've been able to get along. I just came back from the Gestapo and they gave me an International Travel Permit. I intend to go to Switzerland as soon as I can find transport.

He showed me his Permit and I decided to find out more. Jacobson and I parted. I spent the rest of the day wandering around, familiarizing myself with the city. Like many other refugees, I slept in an archway overnight.

Jacobson's parting advice had been to go to the Gestapo and ask for an International Travel Permit. The Gestapo! Into the jaws of the monster! Ridiculous! Dangerous! Impossible! My mood alternated between despair and desperation. I decided to take my chances.

The next day I went to the Gestapo building. The Gestapo was housed in a new building, the former Fascist Party regional headquarters. Many people were milling about in front, or in the vestibule, or were waiting at the foot of the stairs. Most were peasants applying for permits to go to their farms to get food. I waited.

After a while, the door of a first floor office opened. A woman emerged and she walked through the crowd toward the stairs. She looked familiar but I could not place her. I turned to one of the peasants and asked, "Who is this lady?"

"She is the wife of the interpreter."

As she began to ascend the stairs, I decided to take a chance. "Scuse, Signora", I said. "I think I know you."

She stopped, turned to look at me. Then softly I asked, "Have you ever been in Ferramonte?".

There were small signs of embarrassment as she looked at me,

122

coolly and said, "No, signore, I don't know you, you must be mistaken." She turned away and continued up the stairs.

I stayed there another 30 minutes and a man — big tall, heavy set, red cheeks, and green eyes, entered the building and went up the stairs. He too looked familiar. Who was this? The interpreter, I was told.

I left the building wondering whether I had made a mistake, perhaps a dangerous mistake. All afternoon I mulled it over. I could have been mistaken in recognizing one of them but both husband and wife seemed familiar. Who were they? Then I knew: Marek Lazarovich — a man I had known at Ferramonte and his wife Etta. He was a dedicated Communist and we used to have long, involved conversations on politics. What were they doing at the Gestapo headquarters? Had they become collaborators? Or were they spies for the partisans? I decided that they were underground agents.

The next morning I returned to the Gestapo building, asked a few questions of the people waiting outside and learned that the interpreter was expected after one o'clock. I waited in a nearby doorway. At about one o'clock, the interpreter came along the sidewalk heading toward the Gestapo. As he approached, I studied him carefully. Was this Lazarovich? Yes, it was! How would he react? Should I make my approach to him now? As he passed the doorway, I spoke up.

"Lazarovich!", I whispered.

He glanced around him and then looked at me. At first he did not recognize me. Then he spoke softly.

"Doktorzhe, wait in here. Don't talk now. Wait until five o'clock when I leave but don't approach me. Just follow me but not too close". Then he turned and walked away.

I spent the rest of the afternoon wandering through the streets of Chietti. I was in a state of elation. What strange and good fortune. Lazarovich inside the Gestapo! But could he really help me?

At five o'clock I took up my position at the doorway near the Gestapo building. A little after, Lazarovich emerged with another man, an Italian. They walked past me and I followed, about 150 meters behind. The two strolled along, involved in conversation. They walked toward the edge of town and parted with a hand shake.

Lazarovich continued on and I followed. Then he entered a house. I waited for a while, checking that no one was following me. Then I went to the house, opened the door and walked in. Lazarovich greeted me warmly and we kissed. The first thing I had to do was to take a bath for I was full of lice. When I was clean, he gave me a clean shirt.

The Lazarovich's were living modestly in a small second floor apartment. We ate and then reminisced about people and events at Feramante. Lazarovich was a Jew born in Beirut, and raised in Yugoslavia. Etta was from Latvia. He had left Feramante and joined the Partisans. He convinced the Gestapo that he was an anti-partisan Yugoslav. He worked now as an interpreter.

He asked me what made me go to the Gestapo headquarters. I told him about my meeting with Jacobson. Now he became quite pale. "He's still here?", he asked. "The man is stupid and dangerous!" He then told me the story of Jacobson's visit to the Gestapo.

"A week ago Jacobson came to the Gestapo and he recognized my face. Thankfully, he could not remember my name. He talked loudly about Ferramonte. Fortunately, the only person within hearing distance was a young officer who had never heard of Feramante and did not understand what he was talking about. I did not say anything to him. Then he went over to the officer, took out some papers that showed he was an anti-Bolshevik who had fought against the Communists in 1918. The officer gave him travel documents. If he is still in Chietti, the man is a menace to all of us."

We then discussed my future. I thought I might pass myself as a Pole or an Italian.

"You can't remain here," he said. "The Germans are planning to fall back and will make all civilians leave. Before that, everyone in the city will be checked. The Gestapo, not the army, will be checking and you'll certainly be caught. You're a danger to us as well as yourself. Tomorrow, someone will pick you up here and take you out of town. They'll give you new documents." We went to sleep.

The next morning the Lazarovichs left for work and I remained alone until a peasant came to the door. He led me to a farmhouse, not too far away. Several other refugees were there as well. The people gave me a suit to wear.

At noon, Lazarovich arrived. He had new identity papers for me but I needed a photograph quickly. He sent me to a photogarpher — someone who was an underground agent. He took my picture and then accompanied me to the post office, where I lined up to obtain an Identificazione Internationale — an ID used in Europe. It enabled one to use General Delivery. As the woman issued me the card, she made some remarks.

"This is the last card we're issuing. Orders from the Germans. They caught an escaping British prisoner with one of these and they think something's up."

I returned to the farmhouse where my identification papers were completed. I cleaned up again and spent another evening with the Lazarovichs. They were much more relaxed about me now that I looked presentable and had papers.

Two other people were present, a couple anmed D'Allesandro. He was a Chietti merchant.

"You can't stay here", he said. "The Germans will defend the city, force all the civilians out and check everyone's documents. There are two choices. You can go to Rome, easily enough from here. There's a committee at the Vatican that will look after you. But the Germans are still in Rome. Or you can go through the lines to the British side south of here."

Signora D'Allesandro thought that I should try to cross the line. "If you can get through, this will be the best thing for you. You'll be safe there. But there are dangers that you might be caught on the way and that would endanger us here."

Our decision was that I cross the line to the British.

Twice a week organized groups passed over to the British side. The people selected were those who were wanted by the Germans, escaped prisoners, downed flyers, or people wanted by the Germans. Two days after our meeting I was with a group that assembled at a contrada about 15 kilometers south of Chietti. Within the past few days the front line had moved rapidly and was now fairly close to Chietti. Here we were to wait for the right time to move across the line to face the possibilities of either being caught by the Germans, fired on by the British, or liberation.

Chapter 14

THE CROSSING AT CAPOROSSO CEMETERY

During the day our group assembled in a contrada near Chietti. People arrived in ones and twos to avoid drawing the attention of the Germans. I met the leader of the group, a man called Professor Caporalli. He was the brother of the man who had taught me medical pathology in Naples.

In the afternoon, Caporalli came to me and said, "Dottore, I have a surprise for you." He led me into another room where Giovanni Tampoia, a class-mate of mine stood. We embraced adn recounted our experiences since 1940. He had been in the Italian army as a medical officer and deserted immediately after the Italians signed the Armistice. He tried to return to Minervino Murge, a village nearby where his family lived but he was caught by the Germans and ordered to work at the hospital in Chietti.

When he mentioned the Chietti Hospital, I was reminded of Mario's father, the man afflicted with gaseous gangrene. I had suggested that Mario try to get him to the hospital at Chietti. Did he know anything about the case?

"Sure, I know of him. I amputated his leg. He's alive, he left the hospital on crutches. Everybody in the hospital knew of him. When does anyone ever see such a case?" I marvelled at the coincidence that my friend Giovanni had operated on him.

By the end of the day, 20 people had assembled in this contrada, all in one house. We now had enough for a crossing party and we were full of excitement at the prospect of going over to the other side. We awaited our guide. The guide arrived. He was Count Luigi, carrying a huge pistol through his belt. This was the Croat, who had questioned me closely at Tollo, after I had escaped from the Germans. He lectured us crisply on the importance of keeping quiet and obeying instructions without question.

We followed him out into the night, starting in a southerly direction. He led us into the dense woods and through overgrown valleys. Though we were heading generally south we took a tortuous route avoiding roads and paths. We walked for over two hours until we came to a paved road.

Our problem was to cross this road without being seen. German vehicles passed along the road regularly. We had to wait for breaks in the traffic. The traffic was very heavy that night. We lay next to the road for a long while before we could start crossing. Then Count Luigi signalled two people to move across the road. More vehicles came and passed. Then he sent three more across. We waited for Count Luigi to signal another two or three. In small groups we crossed the road until Count Luigi crossed, the last one. It took almost an hour to get all of us across safely.

We continued on. There was little opportunity to rest as the woods were so thick. There was no clear space for more than a few people to sit at one time. Count Luigi was determined to get us to the crossing point as quickly as possible.

We arrived at our rest station at a contrada at about 10:00 p.m., hours earlier than anticipated. We were quite exhausted.

An unexpected complication greeted us. We found another group resting here. They had started out the previous day and should have crossed over last night. As they were an older group of people, they moved slowly and arrived at the rest station too late and tired to continue on as scheduled. They had rested here all day. This other group included Yugoslavs, partisans, British escapees, and a few peasants. They had one woman with them.

We had a problem now. Forty was too many to cross over without detection. Should one group wait until the next night? That was not considered a good idea because the front line was shifting rapidly and the group might be caught by the Germans. The group leaders discussed the problem and decided that they would risk the crossing that night with all 40 people.

At about 2:00 a.m. we started out. The previous group was well rested and found it easy to keep up the brisk pace. Our group had already marched over 30 kilometers that day and we started out very tired. We waded through a stream and through marsh, sinking deeply into the mud with each step.

My friend, Giovanni Tampoia, had a very hard time. He was extremely tired and appeared sick. To make matters worse, he lost a shoe in the muck. We tried to find it but we had to leave off the search because it was necessary to keep moving. After a while, Tamboia had to stop to rest. I waited with him for a few minutes.

"Giovanni, I can't wait any longer", I said. "I'll lose the group."

"You go, I'll wait for the next group", he responded.

Count Luigi came over. "We can't wait for you. As soon as you're rested, go back and wait for another group." Tampoia nodded agreement but no one was certain that there would be another group. "Goodbye and good luck", he said to me cheerfully as we left.

We continued to walk along a country road. Three German soldiers approached. They saw us and we took cover in the brush. But they continued walking as if they did not see us. One of our leaders walked over and handed them something, probably money. Then they continued on down the road.

We entered the village of Caporosso and we walked through it in single file. I was feeling tired and was now at the end of the line. A middle-aged Serb from the previous group kept prodding me to keep up.

"You're a young man, you should be leading the line", he said.

"You rested all day, didn't you", I shot back at him with irritation.

I was annoyed with him but his goading kept me going.

Now we came to the Caporosso Cemetery, the crossing point. The moment of truth. Because of the size of our group we had arrived later than we should have. Dawn was just breaking and the day was lighting up very quickly. The large Cemetery was on a hillside.

The first group went down the hill ahead of us and disappeared from sight. Then we heard the sounds of machine gun fire. While the firing was going on we were told to start down the exposed hillside — in full daylight! The Germans were busy firing at the first group as we descended. When we reached the bottom, we became the targets and machine gun fire burst all around us. We crouched down behind rocks. "Mama mia" was heard repeatedly around me. The firing came from another hill where the Germans had mounted a machine gun.

We tried to size up the situation. There were only a few soldiers. Up the hill ahead of us were some buildings. Germans waiting for us there? The peasants with us were certain that no one occupied the buildings. We started running up the hill fully exposed to machine gun fire. We went up and soon we were out of range. We went past the houses, over the top of the hill and out of view of the Germans.

We counted our numbers. We were all there. No one had been hurt.

Now we saw the Adriatic and the coastal highway. As we walked down the hill we saw some soldiers on the road. They wore red berets and 'CANADA' on shoulder patches. We had succeeded in escaping the Germans.

Chapter 15

RED BERETS AND QUESTIONS

Yes, we had made it. No more German Army around us! Now we were with Canadian soldiers of the British 8th Army. The Canadians brought a truck for us and took us to a small village and placed us in the hands of a British Intelligence unit.

Immediately, they separated the Italians from us — treating them as enemy prisoners. After that they gave us a snack, and interrogated us separately. Who were we? Where had we been? With whom had we been in contact? What papers did we have? They were worried about spies and saboteurs.

I told my story, that I had been the medical officer at a British prisoner camp. They seemed to know of the camp and were familiar with my name. Then they took us to Casoli, a much larger village and we stayed there for a day. They fed us substantial meals — British Army food. I remembered the meagre meals prepared by the peasants in the caves as being tastier than anything I had now. Most of the British Army food came from cans, or was conjured up from powders. They seemed oblivious of the fact that all around them were rich and tasty farm products.

Again we were questioned, the same questions. We were moved to another town and questioned another time. Here we were housed in barracks set up in a stadium. More interrogations. Longer interrogations because they now had files of information on us, mainly notes on our previous interviews. They checked each retelling of our stories for inconsistencies. They also had us elaborate on our observations of the German Army. We were questioned four times in two days.

From my barracks I could see some people working. German prisoners I was told. I was curious about them, to know who they were and what they looked like. A sergeant came into our barracks the next morning.

"We need some people to help out in the kitchen, to peel potatoes", he announced. "Any volunteers?"

I put up my hand. The Sergeant frowned.

"You can't go, doctor", he said. "It's not a doctor's job to peel potatoes."

"I want to because it will give me a chance to take a look at Germans as prisoners, especially after what I've been through with them." The kitchen was near the area where the prisoners were working.

The Sergeant agreed to let me peel potatoes. He lined us up in military fashion and marched us toward the kitchen. As we neared the kitchen, I got a close look at the prisoners. Who do I see? A little fellow, Marchinek, one of the guards as Castelfrantano. This unfortunate fellow was a Pole, whom the Nazis declared to be a German and had conscripted into the Army. Now he was a prisoner.

"Marchinek", I shouted as I ran over to where he was working. We embraced and exchanged greetings in Polish. "What are you doing here?", I asked.

"Doctorzhe, you remember you told me to escape, the first chance I get. Well, I did."

The Sergeant intervened and separated us. He was very

disturbed by this scene and reported it. Naturally, I was sent for further interrogation.

I spent an hour with an intelligence officer, telling Marchinek's story in detail. Then they called Marchinek in and grilled him for several hours. By the end of the day they removed him from the German prisoner group and sent him to the Polish Corps of the 8th Army. Marchinek was now a Pole again!

We stayed in the stadium a few days more. Some of our group were questioned further but I was interrogated no more. We were put on a train, heading south to Bari, where the British maintained a large refugee camp. Most of the people on the train were German and Italian prisoners and there was an armed guard on each car including our own.

The train stopped at Foggia in the afternoon and remained there until 9 o'clock. We wanted to walk around a bit and asked permission to leave. Our guard told us the city was deserted and patrolled by the Americans. As we had no papers, we would have trouble if the Americans found us. Three of us decided to take our chances because we longed for a good plate of Italian macaroni. The city was largely empty with only a few houses occupied. But we did find a restaurant that was closed. We knocked on the door, the door opened and we asked for a meal. The food was a great disappointment. We then wandered about the empty streets.

Suddenly, a jeep screeched to a halt in front of us. "Who are you? Where are you going?" I started to explain in my limited English but they were not interested in answers. They ordered us into the jeep, took us to their headquarters and started to book us as prisoners.

"What do you mean, prisoners?", I asked.

"You've got no documents. We don't know who you are", the officer said.

Then a soldier, an Italian-American, came over and spoke with us in Italian. "What do you think you are doing?", he asked. "You don't have any papers. You could be German spies."

"Come to the train, the British soldiers will identify us", we said.

Dr. Salim Diamand

They held a conference and decided to take us by jeep to the station. As soon as we arrived at the station the British soldiers began laughing at us. The Italian speaking American explained to us that we would have been placed in a group of prisoners that were headed to the U.S. in a few days. We got on the train and waited for it to move that evening.

Our train moved slowly through the night. We arrived in Bari the next morning and were sent to a large refugee camp — the Carbonara, a camp built by the Italians to hold Allied prisoners. Now it housed over a thousand refugees in barracks with two and three tiered bunks.

We had to be interrogated once again. The interrogator had a file in front of him that had grown very thick. It contained the reports of the previous interrogations and some information about my life before the war. When the inquiry was completed, we were given identity cards and we were free to go almost anywhere outside the camp. They also gave us British Army uniforms without any insignia. I still wore my Luftwaffe boots.

The camp population was a mixture of people from Africa, the Middle East and all parts of Europe. A Russian, Pavel, who had been taken prisoner by the Germans and then escaped, turned up here. At that time everyone admired the Russian Army which was now smashing the Germans. We treated Pavel as a hero and a celebrity. He, naturally, enjoyed the adulation. However, a few weeks later several other Russians arrived and the rumour spread that Pavel was a deserter. One morning he tried to hang himself, was cut down and taken to the hospital still alive. He survived the suicide attempt, but was handed over to the Russians and never heard from again.

The camp was placed under the control of the UNRRA, United Nation Refugee Rehabilitation Agency. As most of the refugees were Jews, the Joint Distribution Committee came as well. We had visits by soldiers of the Jewish Brigade of the British army, units made up of soldiers from Palestine.

At Passover the Jewish Brigade organized a massive Seder. Thousands of people — refugees, Jewish soldiers from the American, British an Polish armies — sat down to a festive meal

134

celebrating the Exodus from Egypt. We had matzos, kreplach and fefillte fish — foods that I had not tasted since I left Poland in 1935. It was a sad reminder of family that had vanished. We were deeply moved, some of us to tears, as we read the story of the Exodus and heard the speeches by Army officers and representatives of Jewish organizations.

I wanted to go home, to Bolechov in Poland, to find out what had happened to my family. I considered approaching the Russian Consul for a permit. I really knew very little about the extent of the destruction of European Jewry and was naive. The Jewish Brigade soldiers ended my innocence. They knew a great deal and told me what I could expect. One of them, Manis Gyelki, was from my city, Bolechov. He and his family had emigrated to Palestine in 1930. He had information about the fate of the Bolechov Jews. I knew now that to go to Poland was to visit a graveyard.

I was at loose ends as to what to do with myself. I considered joining the Polish Corps and had a serious discussion about it with a man named Chaikoff who was serving the Polish forces. After our talk, he returned to his unit at Monte Cassino and participated in the final assault and capture by the Poles. Finally, I decided to return to Naples, a place I remembered as being a very happy part of life.

I was free to go where I wanted in Italy, at least the part not occupied by the Germans. However, transport was not easy to find because everything was reserved for the military. The Palestinians came to my aid and drove me by truck to Naples. I spent my first few weeks in a house maintained by the Jewish Brigade for refugees, many waiting to go to Palestine.

Now I felt ready to take up my life where it had stopped in 1940. The prison camps, the hiding and pretenses were over.

Chapter 16

RETURN TO NAPLES

Naples, April 1944. Here, in a shelter provided by the men of the Jewish Brigade, I had an all but forgotten luxury — a bedroom to myself. No more barrack-rooms, nor sharing a cave or farmhouse floor. It was a tiny room, but mine, for the time being. Naples was beautiful and sunny at that time of year. It was also crowded with soldiers, refugees from the concentration camps and evacuees from the battle zones.

The war was still with us and we were reminded harshly of it two nights after I arrived. The air raid alarms sounded — a German air attack. Everyone in the house ran to the shelter, all except another man and I. We listened to the anti-aircraft batteries firing away and the drone of airplanes in the distance. My companion became concerned and decided to head for the shelter. As he went out the door and down the outside stair case some anti-aircraft debris came down upon him, almost at the same time as the firing stopped and the all-clear sounded. He was badly wounded in the thigh and arm, and an artery was cut. I had heard him cry out and came down immediately to find him bleeding profusely. Using string, I applied a tourniquet and stopped the bleeding. He lay there, asked for a cigarette and smoked until an ambulance came and took him to a hospital. He died the next morning.

I wanted to resume my life in Naples, taking up where I had left off, but this was not as easy as I had thought. Many of my friends and acquaintances were no longer there. Some had died. Many, I was told, had been in the Italian Army and were trapped in the north, still held by the Germans. Finally, I found one friend, a dentist named Eisenberg. He came from Rumania originally, had been in France, and we met when he arrived in Italy a year after I settled in Naples.

Eisenberg roomed in the house of one of the professors, and married the professor's daughter. He had converted to Catholicism. Eisenberg welcomed me warmly when I showed up at his door. He asked me about myself and listened to my story. My situation was very much a contrast to his war experience. He had completed his studies in dentistry, married, set up a practice and he had not been bothered in any way as a foreigner or a Jew. He had lived through the war, no better or worse than any other Neapolitan. Surprisingly, he mentioned the names of several others with the same experience.

When I heard this, I questioned why I and the others had been rounded up, placed in camps, or lived in hiding, while others were almost untouched. I can only explain it as the total arbitrariness of unrestricted authority which allows rulers to act on whim.

Eisenberg wanted me to stay with him and his family, his wife and two children. I declined his offer, for I felt it would only help me put off some important decisions about my future work and living arrangements. I was determined to find work immediately.

I remembered a good friend and classmate, Lorenzo Scafuri, who came from a village, Baiano, near Naples. As there was no phone connection, I took the train one afternoon and presented myself at his door. His father, Matteo, a lean, sad looking man met me. His face lighted up when I introduced myself.

"Dottore, Lorenzo is not here, he's in a prison camp in Germany. Please come in."

I spent the evening with him and he asked me to stay overnight. He had suffered a great deal. He had three sons. One was killed in a hunting accident, another in the war and Lorenzo a prisoner somewhere in Germany, at the Russian front. The next morning as I was preparing to leave, he put an arm around me.

"Why leave?", he asked. "You can stay here and when Lorenzo comes back, you can practice together. I am all alone here and would love to hve you."

I explained that I was just starting in Naples. Actually, I wanted to be in the big city and it was time that I was on my own.

I wanted to find a medical position. I went to the American Army headquarters and obtained an interview with a Colonel. I told him of my experiences. He was very sympathetic but could not help me in any way directly. But he did give me his card and told me to use it in any way that might help me find work.

I went to visit Professor Di Guglielmo, who was head of the Emergency Services and Dean of Medicine at the University. He was also a renowned lecturer on pathology. In fact, a disease of the blood is called — Malatia Di Guglielmo. Experienced doctors came from all over Italy to hear his lectures, even his lectures to students. When I was a student, I had to come early to assure myself a seat whenever he lectured. The Professor interviewed me.

"There's not much I can offer anyone. We lost the war and there isn't much money around for staff", he explained. "But you're a graduate of our university and seem like a fine fellow. I can offer you a job in the research institute with a very small salary. In time you might be able to advance."

The prospect of scientific research did not interest me at this time. After all of my experiences of the past few years I wanted something closely related to the life around me. I told him that I would think about it. I then went to the American Army hospital that had been set up on Vomero in the Vanvitelli School, presented them with my documents and the Colonel's card and was immediately hired as a lab technician. I took a room nearby in Piazza Medalia D'Oro.

This job lasted only a few weeks becaue I could not get along with the Sergeant, a man who knew nothing about the work but insisted on handing out orders in the most imperious and insulting manner possible. Finally, I spoke up in anger. Two days later I was dismissed.

For several weeks I was without work and was supported by funds supplied by a refugee service organization. Each day I went out looking for work and met many people, Americans and Italians. I became acquainted with an American sergeant named Gedalli, a Chiropractor. I had never heard the term before as the profession did not exist anywhere in Europe. He convinced me that the was some kind of medical practitioner just short of a physician. He asked a favour of me.

"I would like to go into the last year of medicine and become fully qualified," he said. "As you are a graduate, perhaps, you could talk to the Dean. With your help, I am sure he'll admit me."

Naively, I went to see the Dean again. "Idiot", he roared with laughter. "Tell him that we might let him enroll in the first year, if he wants." I returned to tell my friend who was incredulous that the Dean would treat an American this way.

My work at the American hospital did lead to some strange results. One day a soldier who I had met at the hospital approached me.

"I've been looking for you", he said. "I have a friend who needs some shots. We'll give you the penicillin. Will you inject it?"

I had learned about this drug only recently. "What's his condition?", I asked.

"He's got gonhorrea", he answered. "If he goes to the Army doctors, it will go on his record."

I agreed. The next day he showed up with his friend and some penicillin. I administered 10,000 units each day. (Today the bacteria have become resistant and one must administer 500,000 units.) My payment was penicillin, a drug that was unavailable outside military hospitals and in great demand as a "wonder drug".

Now, I found myself with a small medical practice. The soldier brought more of his comrades for treatment at least once a week. He had turned his contact with me into a business. His payments of penicillin helped me to live for the next month.

I met a British medical officer, who hearing that I had a year of tropical disease studies, told me that a place was available at a malaria field unit near Rome, which had been liberated recently. He arranged for me to have the position and soon I was on my way. I was not anxious to leave Naples but the malaria unit offered me the opportunity to practice medicine in a regular way. However, I chose to keep paying rent on my room in Naples, because it was uncertain how long the job would last.

The train to Rome stopped at one point to pick up passengers. From the window I could see a huge landscape of devastation extending up the mountainside. Remnants of buildings, shattered vehicles, craters and on top of the mountain the ancient monestary lay in ruins. This was Cassino, the bitterest and bloodiest battlefield in Italy. I thought of the soldiers of the Polish Corps that I had met at the Passover Seder in Bari, who returned to their units to participate in the final assault and capture of the monestary.

The British malaria unit was located in Rome, but I did my work out in the nearby villages where malaria was rampant. I lived in Rome, renting a room from a widow whose husband had been in the army, but she had not heard from him for more than a year. She understood that he was a prisoner but did not know where. It was a pleasant place and I had breakfast and supper there every day.

I spent most of my time examining and treating children who were afflicted with malaria and developed enlarged spleens. After a few weeks, I learned that the unit was soon to close down. I decided to return to Naples. And because of this experience with children I wanted to study pediatrics.

Dr. Salim Diamand

I was driven back to Naples by jeep. As we approached the city, I realized how fond I was of the city and its people. I especially liked the food there. Neapolitans! Whether eating at home or in restaurants Neapolitans always had fresh meats and vegetables. They turned their noses up at canned foods and frozen meats. Neapolitans preferred to do without, if they could not have fresh foods.

I went back to Professor Di Guglielmo to discuss my plans. However, I was not prepared to be a full-time post-graduate student. The Dean agreed to recommend me to Professor Auricchio, the chief of Pediatrics. Shortly after that, I was enrolled.

My day began at 8:00 a.m. when we spent the morning at the Pediatric Clinic on Piazza Santaniello, attending lectures, assisting the Professor or his assistants in the treatment of children. The clinic saw large numbers of children from the south who were suffering from Malaria and Leishmania. Leishmania is a disease caused by protozoa in the water. In both situations, the chidlren came to us with extremely enlarged spleens. We treated them with an anitmonium solution.

I left my small room in the Medalia D'Orio and took a small apartment on the Via Enrico Alvino, not far from the clinic. The apartment — one bedroom, kitchen and bathroom — served as an office and living quarters. I put a shingle outside and waited for patients. The waiting was brief for Naples was short of doctors. Many doctors had gone into the Italian Army and when the war ended, the Germans quickly pressed them into their medical services. Many Neapolitan doctors were trapped in Norther Italy, serving with the Germans, the Partisans or just hiding out behind the lines. The war was still on and we were reminded of it every so often when German planes flew and dropped bombs. One building near mine was destroyed by a German bomb. Fortunately no one was killed.

I saw very sick people and had limited resources for treating them. Few drugs were available. Sulfa was in ample supply and sometimes we had penicillin. I tried to reestablish contact with the Sergeant who had supplied me with penicillin but he had been transferred. One of my first cases was a boy who had contracted typhoid along with perforated intestines, periostitus, and meningitis. We treated him with penicillin and sulfa. He started with a very poor prognosis but recovered after a long period of treatment.

Another of my early patients was a well-known artist whose paintings hung in galleries throughout Europe. He was suffering from Colitis and had been to many doctors before and they had failed to help him. Most had diagnosed his condition as largely psychological. As soon as he came to see me, he handed me a diary, 1000 pages detailing his condition day by day, treatment by treatment and doctor by doctor, with his comments on all of the physicians who had treated him. It was largely a catalogue of complaints and accusations against the medical profession. I was fearful of how I would turn out in his jottings. I managed to help him find a measure of relief from his sufferings and he rewarded me with several paintings.

I had now begun to make a modest living as a physician, the first time I had ever really supported myself at my profession. I found a few old friends and made many new ones. The reemergence of political parties added another interest for me. A new life opened for me.

Chapter 17

WAITING FOR THE END

My apartment-home now became the centre of my life. My practice grew steadily. Patients did not make appointments but dropped in at almost any time — early in the morning on their way to work, in the evening on their way home, in the middle of the night, if something bothered them. When I went out for a while, several patients might be waiting at my door when I returned.

Payment of fees was not a simple matter, because of shortages and rampant inflation. I preferred not to receive Lire but did if there was no other way for the patient to pay. Most people brought me food, clothing, or other goods. Almost any type of food or commodity had value and could be traded in Naples at that time, as almost everything that people wanted was in short supply. Lire had to be turned into commodities quickly before the money lost value and a great deal of time was spent in exchanging an item for something I needed, for example, a jacket, a pair of shoes, or whatever.

My apartment also became a social centre for many people. I became acquainted with many American soldiers stationed in Naples and they, like my patients, dropped in at almost any time. They welcomed some place to come to besides the usual soldier's haunts and they liked the idea that they could meet some "real" Italians.

My place was always full of people and buzzing with activity. Sometimes it seemed like a continuous party, as well as a medical practice. I might be examining a patient in one room, while a group of people might be singing, arguing, drinking, feasting or conversing in the other room.

Politics was the primary interest of most of my Italian friends. While the war continued, political parties were banned. But every one was straining at the bit and the parties existed unofficially. The people who gathered in my apartment were mostly Communists and Socialists, with a few Christian Democrats. They argued over fine points of ideology. One aim that united them was an end to the Monarchy and to create a Republic. They talked about the practical measures needed to rid Italy of its king. Out on the streets, anti-Monarchist graffiti appeared, demanding a Republic.

One day a friend took me aside. "Diamand, be careful", he warned, "you're going to get into trouble. The police are keeping a dossier on you. They're taking the names of the communists who come here. Somebody's reporting on you. Remember you're not an Italian citizen."

I did not take the warning seriously for I had been through worse situations during the previous few years.

The war in Europe finally ended on May 8, 1945. All Naples celebrated. I joined with the throngs in the centre of the city. I wandered into a Port Alba Pizzaria that I used to frequent before the war and the proprietor recognized me and treated me to a meal. We all felt relieved and looked forward to a period of peace and rebirth.

Chapter 18

STARTING AGAIN IN NAPLES

With the end of the war, politics returned to Italy with intensity. Neapolitans had never been enthusiastic about Fascism. Indeed Mussolini understood this and rarely visited Naples.

Tolgiati returned from his exile in Russia to head the Communist Party and he received a tumultuous welcome in Italy. The Communists showed surprising strength everywhere in the country. I was acquainted with many of the Communist leaders in Naples. The party became active in providing social and medical services to people. Though I was not a member of the Party, I joined one of their medical teams that went into the poor districts of the city and the villages to give ambulatory medical services. The dedication of the rank and file of the Party was impressive and their willingness to give their time to community service was without parallel in Italy at that time.

In my contacts with the Party people I met Tolgiati. I also met the Viviani brothers, who were prominent in arts; one brother, Rafae, had founded the Neapolitan Theatre; Sconamiglio, the distinguished professor and Numeroso, the writer were among my acquaintances.

Few Italians knew of the realities of the Holocaust except in broadest terms. A Jew, a former Polish soldier, gave me a copy of a Polish newspaper that contained a long article about Treblinka. I translated it into Italian and it was published in a left-wing journal, La Voce. It may have been the first article of its kind to be published in Italy.

One former soldier was a struggling artist, who was having a hard time selling any of his work that were being displayed in a small gallery. I met one of the Viviani brothers, an art critic and asked him to mention the artist in one of his articles. Viviani visited the exhibition and wrote a laudatory critique. The next time I met the artist, I learned that he had sold all his paintings to one purchaser who had read Viviani's article.

On May 3rd, 1944, I was appointed as a Medical Officer of Health for the City of Naples. I and my other medical colleagues were trying to restore an adequate level of public health to the city after the War. We were very concerned to identify people who were carriers of communicable diseases and we would then verify their illness, isolate them and then treat them.

The first district of Naples I was assigned to was Forcella, a densely-packed slum of poor people. The buildings were infested with vermin of every type. The people, however, were simple and easy to deal with.

Forcella was one of the celebrated slums of Europe, a den of vice and crimes of all kind. Its thieves and confidence men held the highest reputations — they could steal the clothes off your back and sell it back to you before you knew what had happened. In Forcella one could buy almost anything and it was also the centre of black market activity. However, things purchased were not always what they seemed. American cigarettes, for example, always in great demand, could be purchased. But, as often as not, the cigarettes would turn out to have a flavouring of tobacco on the ends and sand or horse manure in between. The shams and scams of Forcello were legendary. I developed a trusting relationship with the residents and found that among themselves they were a helping, considerate and cooperative population. Having gained their trust, I was successful in winning their cooperation in improving health conditions. I was able to get some of the volunteer doctors, usually Communists, to give free medical service. I was never a victim of any of the hoaxes they perpetrated on other outsiders.

I needed hospital experience to complete my work in pediatrics and the Professor Tatafiore recommended me to a hospital run by the Order of Santa Maria D'Egypto. I spent every morning there. The Mother Superior, Domitillo, was from Milan and like many northerners, she did not like southern Italians. She and Professor Tatafiore did not get along. However, she seemed to favour me and saw to it that each day I had an especially good lunch at the hospital, better than any provided to Tatafiore, whenever he was present. She made a great show of her favourtism for me. Tatafiore would needle her with, "Mother Domitille, he will convert you to Judaism before you'll convert him to Christianity". While working for the City of Naples, I was thus able to complete all my training in pediatrics.

Chapter 19

DECIDING ON MY FUTURE

The war had ended. I had a marginal existence in Naples. But what should I do? Should I stay in Italy? Should I immigrate? I myself did not know. I had a sister in the United States and she wanted me to emigrate to the U.S. I thought that, perhaps, I should go to Palestine. I also had a cousin who was urging me to join him in Paris. I simply waited, uncertain about my future.

By 1945, Naples had now become the assembly and embarcation point for many illegal immigarnts trying to emigrate to Palestine against the wishes of the British. Under the noses of the British in Italy, the Jewish underground organized groups and provided military training to those war survivors who were waiting for a chance to flee Europe and emigrate illegally to Palestine. I would see these small freighters leaving Naples and the nearby harbours with these survivors heading for Palestine.

I had, by now, reestablished my life in Naples. I also enjoyed

Dr. Salim Diamand

participating, like all other Italians, in the revitalization of political life. I and all my friends got caught up in the forthcoming elections which were to be held in June, 1946. All parties tried to outdo each other — the Christian Democrats, the Republicans, the Socialists, the Communists. Politics, like most other things in Italy, is a public sport. Almost every night, I and my friends would be out, politicing and propagandizing. We would even go out and paint the sidewalks as an aspect of politicing. I remember, in particular, one of these nights, we had a big party. We took a fiacre, a horse-drawn coach, and we went to Puzzeoli, then around Vesuvius, then to many other villages. We had a friend there and he had a retaurant and he prepared a dinner. We ate maybe ten beautiful dishes and drank excessively. The elections confirmed the end of the Monarchy for Italy and established the Republic.

After the election, somebody approached me and said, "Diamand, do you intend to immigrate or do you intend to stay here?" I didn't know myself, I didn't know what to do, what to decide.

I decided to wait, but in order to wait, I wanted to be affiliated with some organization involved with immigration. In the summer of 1946, I was approached by a Jewish Agency, JIAS, which was associated with UNRRA, with a question. Would I accept to be a doctor in a refugee camp? I pondered and I said, "But, I have a place in Naples and I'm working." I had a friend from the past who was a naturalized Italian, his name was Eisenberg, Giacomo. He lived through the war without being touched by the Italians, in spite of the fact that he was Jewish. Indeed, he had converted. "Listen, Diamand", Eisenberg said, "I will tell you one thing, you better go. You participated in the elections and you better go now if they offer you a job with UNRRA."

UNRRA was deeply involved in relief work, especially with Holocaust survivors who were coming to a variety of refugee camps in Italy, in transit for the United States, Canada, Australia and even Palestine. I was offered the position of Camp Doctor at one of these camps, Cremona. August, 1946 — I left Naples for a new career as a Camp Doctor.

I arrived in Cremona in the evening. I was told that I would be taken to the refugee camp the next day, but that I would spend the night in the Palazzo Farinacci, a magnificent palazzo, with luxurious bedrooms, crystal, mirrors, paitings. What an irony of history, to spend the night in such surroundings!

The refugee camp was made up predominantly of Jews who had somehow survived the extermination camps. The trains with these Holocaust survivors were arriving night and day, each with some 300-400 refugees. Many arrived dazed, dressed in rags, emaciated corpses. Everyone had to be processed, then examined, then disinfected. After this, they received new certificates.

The stories we were told were horrendous. It was not possible for anyone to comporehend the terror, the horror. My brain simply closed down in disbelief.

One day, towards the end of 1946, I was summoned by the Senior Medical Officer of the camp, a lady Doctor from California, Dr. Barclay. "You know, Dr. Diamand, I am very sorry. I have to tell you something...you have to leave this camp. You are being transferred to another camp." I refused to go. "I am not going. I am not a refugee. I am Jewish like all the others, but I am not a refugee. I live here, I have working papers. I am a former Medical Officer for the City of Naples. I have not just arrived here from Poland, or from some German extermination camp."

"You must help out, now. We will make you the Senior Medical Officer and increase your pay, if you agree. But you must go to Rivoli."

"But what is Rivoli?" I asked.

"Rivoli is another refugee camp, mostly Jews. The Senior Medical Officer there had somehow helped the Nazis. The refugees found out about this, surrounded his house and they wanted to kill him. You must help us out — now."

The next day, Dr. Barclay and I drove from Cremona to Milan to meet with the Director of UNRRA. His name was Dr. Wheatfield, I think. He himself had been a prisoner in a Japanese prison camp and he wrote a pamphlet about the lack of vitamins in the diet. Between the coaxing of Drs. Barclay and Wheatfield, I agreed to accept the position at Rivoli.

Rivoli is a town about 50 kilometres from Turin in the pre-alpine region of Italy. I spent the evening before my actual arrival in the camp at the Hotel of the Three Kings. There, I was met and briefed by Captain Scott, a tall, moustached Scotsman.

Rivoli was a large refugee camp of some 2000 people. They were mostly young people who had seen their families exterminated and destroyed during the war. Almost all of them wanted to go to Palestine as it was then called. We used to do routine medical treatments in the camp. When we required accesss to a hospital, we would go to Gruliasko, a town slightly east of the location of the camp. Major medical problems were taken care of in Turino. The refugees who had been processed to go to the United States used to go first to Naples, then on from there. However, many of the refugees were being recruited to join the "Palmach".

Part of the camp's activities was attending the soccer matches in Turino. The camp administrators would arrange for tickets and for a truck to take people down to the matches. We also met many of the players who went on to become famous in European soccer, such as Mr. Mazzola. He and others used to come and visit the refugee camp. Mazzola, who died tragically in a plane crash, had his younger son with him when he visited us. The young boy went on to become one of the most accomplished of Italy's players, as well.

By the beginning of 1948, the camp started to decline in numbers. Most of the people left for Israel, others went off to South America, while still others departed for the United States.

I was transferred, yet again, to a camp named Trani, a little city of about 30,000 people in the southeast of Italy on the Adriatic coast, about 40 kilometres from Bari. This camp had about 2,000 refugees, again, mostly Jews who intended to emigrate to Palestine. The medical Chief of the camp was Dr. Raftos. The surgeon in the hospital was Dr. Kuharik, who emigrated to Canada. One day, we received a call from Rome asking if we could provide a medical doctor to accompany a group of immigrants to Australia. I was asked if I wanted to go. I agreed. By the time I had arranged some of my personal affairs, such as going to Bari to get some money from my bank, we received a telegram from Rome informing me that they did not need me any longer.

Many of the cases we had to treat in the camp at Trani were more of a psychological or mental nature, than physical. For many of these problems, we called upon the medical doctors from the University of Bari. We also had delegates from Palestine who used to screen the refugees who wanted to emigrate to Palestine.

One day, I was approached by one of these delegates. "Dr. Diamand, listen, this morning, try to be away from the camp. We have here a lady whom we suspect was a German collaborator. We intend to take her to Israel. No doubt, she will find good reasons for declining to go to Israel. But with you absent from the camp, there will be no legitimate medical reason why she cannot be selected to go to Israel."

I returned to the camp around six o'clock in the evening. Upon my return, I was told to go away again, it was not time to return. A few hours later, in the night I returned to the camp. I was told that she had left. She was going to stand trial in Israel.

Life in camp Trani was full of many strange and ironic episodes. Once, one of the Italian camp police came to me and called out, "Dottore." He went into one of the small offices and before he entered, he winked at me — to follow him. I did. He then handed me a letter. I opened it and it was a letter from the Rabbi of Rome addressed to the camp Doctor of Trani. I read the letter. It said that the man, now standing in front of me, had converted to Judaism. He was now circumcised but that he required medication. I administered what was required, but then I turned to him. "You are crazy. Why have you converted to Judaism? Look around you. This place and many other camps are full of misery, horrified and tortured Jews. The only reason they were persecuted is that they are Jews. Do you now convert so that you too can be exterminated in the next Holocaust?"

Dr. Salim Diamand

He responded. "Listen, I fell in love with a girl from Rumania. She is going to Israel. I want to join her, but she will not let me unless I am a Jew. So, I converted." He left.

A few months later, I met my friend Capitano Alessi, the Police superintendant. I had not seen him for some time. I asked him about the policeman, who had converted. What happened to him? Alessi told me that he did emigrate to Israel with the Rumanian girl. A short time after they arrived, she left him. It also turned out that she was not even Jewish. She was Rumanian but had wanted to flee from the Eastern zone, so she said she was Jewish. Apparently, the Israeli authorities sent her back to Rumania.

Throughout the year 1949, this camp, like the ones I had worked in the previous few years, was getting smaller and smaller. Most people were leaving for Israel. Others, for the United States, others for Chile. One person left for Canada. Finally, in early 1950, the camp was closed down and I was transferred to Bagnioli. This was a large camp near Naples from where most people went on to Australia or the United States. It was one of the few remaining camps still operating. I was appointed the Senior Medical Officer of the hospital. I used to spend a lot of time in Naples. During one of my visits, I went to see my old friend Eisenberg. "Listen, Diamand, I think you had better try to emigrate. I don't think there is much left for you here."

I wanted to stay in Italy. I knew no other place, really. I had been here for more than a decade by now. Naples was my home. Napoli was my temperament. I knew the culture. I did not know what to do again.

Chapter 20

THE EMIGRATION

In 1950, I continued to work as a Medical Officer for UNRRA. I was based in Bagnioli and I also worked in three small transit camps all in the province of Ancona — Senigalia, Fermo and Iesi. Our major concerns were the younger children in these camps. Most of these refugees were destined to emigrate to Austraila. But the Australian authorities insisted that everyone had to be immunized with gama globoulin to avoid the possible acquisition of measles before they could embark.

By now, it was more than four years after the end of the war. Everyone was trying to get out of these camps, to emigrate somewhere. Many had already left after being processed to emigrate to various countries. But for those who still remained, they had spent more than four years in the conditions of uncertainty about their future. They all wanted to simply get out — anywhere, wherever they had friends or relatives, sponsors or invitations.

157

I had a sister in New York. So, like all the others, I decided that I would apply for immigration to the United States. In order to do so, I had to go to Rome, to the Cinecita. This was the place that Mussolini had built to imitate Hollywood, to become the focus of the cinema industry in Italy. It was then being used as a major clearing-house for transits, for those who were applying for immigration. I had to fill out the required documents, but I didn't know, quite, how to do it. I approached the Senior Medical Officer whose name was Mirko Skofic, who also happened to be the husband of Gina Lollobrigida, for assistance.

I then returned to Naples to await the decision. I had a wonderful friend at the time, a nurse who was also a British subject. She had an invitation to emigrate to Canada. We made a farewell party for her and then I accompanied her to her ship. She told me that I should do everything possible to get to the United States or Canada and that she would wait for me. Yet another one of my ties in Italy was departing.

Alone, I returned to my apartment and lay down. What was I going to do? What would happen to me? Would my application for entry to the United States be accepted, or not? Should I stay on as a transit camp doctor? Should I continue to work at Bagnioli?

It was very early morning, no more than four or five hours after I had accompanied my friend to her ship which was to take her to Canada. The door to my apartment opened. It was my friend...she said that she didn't want to emigrate without me. She had left the ship to return to ensure that I would accompany her.

I had not had a response to my application for emigration to the United States that I had filed in Rome. I filed another application with the United States Consulate in Naples. Again, I waited and waited, No response. My life was in limbo. I continued to work as a Medical Officer at the camp in Bagnioli, under the auspices of UNRRA. But, sooner or later, I knew that something would happen.

"Doctor Diamand, Doctor Diamand, Immigration wants to see you." That was the sound coming over the camp loudspeaker system that I was waiting for. I went to the Immigration Office.

There, an Officer from UNRRA informed that there was an opening in the Royal Columbian Hospital in New Westminster, British Columbia, Canada. "Do you accept?". "Sure", I said.

I filed my application immediately. In a week, I received a phone call. I had to go to Rome, to the Canadian Embassy to process my Passport and my visa to Canada. It was a Thursday. I shall never forget it. The next day, Friday, I told my friend, Annie, "We're going to Rome, to get my visa and then, we will be off to Canada."

The visa offices were packed with people, mostly Italians applying to emigrate to join their relatives in Canada. There were very few camp refugees applying for entry into Canada. I had been given references by UNRRA and I answered the few questions put to me easily. My visa was issued. I was then told, "It's best if you leave for Canada as soon as possible."

That was Friday. The next day, Saturday, I inquired if there was a passage available soon for Canada. I was told that there was one scheduled to leave the next day, Sunday. I had the money, booked two fares. My fate was sealed.

On Sunday, at 4:00 p.m., Annie and I left for Canada.

I was scared. I was leaving my life behind me. I was cutting myself off from Naples, from the people, the environment, the things which I had gotten to know so well and to love so much. All I knew was that I was leaving everything which was familiar, but I did not know what I should expect.

The passage to Canada was good. We arrived in St. John's. My first impression of Canada was that an Immigration Officer boarded our ship with a very large Labrador. To me, it looked like a very large black calf, a peaceful calf. It sniffed at me. I always think of this first encounter with Canada — a large, beautiful Labrador, Canada's emissary greeting me to this peaceful country.

The date was December 6, 1950. I was in Canada — Europe was behind me, at last!

Dr. Salim Diamand